Sacramental
Living

Sacramental Living

Falling Stars & Coloring Outside the Lines

Dwight W. Vogel &
Linda J. Vogel

UPPER
ROOM BOOKS

NASHVILLE

Unless otherwise stated, scripture quotations are from the New Revised Standard Version Bible, copyright © 1989 by the Division of Christian Education of the National Council of the Churches of Christ in the U.S.A. Used by permission.

Scripture quotations identified AP are the author's paraphrase.

Text to "Give Thanks to the Source" by Ruth Duck, copyright © 1997. Used by permission.

Story by Barbara Dust is used here with her permission.

Expert from letter by Houston McKelvey is reprinted with his permission.

Excerpt from "Thanksgiving Over the Water" from *The United Methodist Book of Worship*, © 1992 by The United Methodist Publishing House. Reprinted by permission of the publisher.

Excerpt from "Joseph Cardinal Bernardin: Reflection on his life and his death" by Kathleen Hughes is used here with her permission.

Excerpts from Baptismal Covenant I and Baptismal II from *The United Methodist Book of Worship*, © 1992 by The United Methodist Publishing House. Reprinted by permission of the publisher.

Excerpts on pages 67, 120–121 are from the English translation of the *Exsultet* from *The Roman Missal* © 1973, International Committee on English in the Liturgy, Inc (ICEL). All rights reserved.

The Upper Room Web Site: http://www.upperroom.org

Cover Design: John Robinson
Cover Illustration:© Alan E. Cober/SIS
First Printing: 1999

Library of Congress Cataloging-in-Publication Data

Vogel, Dwight.
    Sacramental living: falling stars and coloring outside the lines
    /Dwight W. Vogel and Linda J. Vogel.
        p.   cm.
    Includes bibliographical references.
    ISBN 0-8358-0889-0
    1. Christian life—Methodist authors.   I. Vogel, Linda Jane.
    II. Title.
    BV4501.2.V58B   1999
    248.4—dc21   99-11111
                                                            CIP
Printed in the United States of America

To Aunt Esther
whose deep faith and self-giving love
have blessed so many for more
than ninety-eight years

TABLE OF CONTENTS

PREFACE

During the fall of 1997, we were scholars in residence at the Institute for Ecumenical and Cultural Research. We came to immerse ourselves in Benedictine prayer life and to work together on a book about sacramental living. We sought to slow down, to regain a rhythm of living that included hard work, regular prayer and worship, exercise, re-creation and rest. Here at St. John's Abbey and University, and St. Benedict's Monastery and College, with Benedictine hospitality, lakes and woods, libraries and chapels, we have a wonderful place to write, to pray, and to be.

When we came, we knew we wanted to write about sacramental living. For us, that meant taking everyday life seriously and discovering ways the church's worship intersects and penetrates our daily journey.

Twenty-five years ago, we spent nine months at the Ecumenical Institute. We were blessed then by learning from Sister Jeremy Hall, OSB. Now she is fulfilling her vocation as a hermit of her community. Being able to share with and learn from her again this year, is a gift we treasure. She led her community's retreat last year. In preparation, she spent a whole year being "marinated in scripture"—reflecting on the questions God and Jesus ask: "Where are you?" "Who do you say that I am?" "Can you drink the cup?" "Do you love me?"

"Being marinated" is a metaphor that helps us as we reflect on sacramental living. We seek to discern sacramental dynamics in our experiences of God's grace and the call to discipleship. What does it mean to "talk the talk" and "walk the walk" of faith?

We spent an hour visiting with Abbot Timothy Kelly, OSB in his office. We talked about what it means to live sacramentally. What are the pitfalls? What fosters sacramental living? We learned he worked for six months with The Upper Room and was deeply blessed as he shared with United Methodists and others. What joy it is for us to be blessed by being in this Benedictine community of prayer and work, and to send the fruits of our labors to The Upper Room for publication.

As weeks here passed, we found ourselves drawn again and again to St. Benedict's Monastery. We were always welcomed, supported, and nourished by the sisters' deep and unassuming spirituality, and by the careful attention they give to prayer and worship in Sacred Heart Chapel. We cannot begin to list all the sisters who have blessed us, but to Sister Ephrem Hollermann, OSB, their prioress, and to the entire community, we say "thank you."

We believe that story is basic to understanding sacramental living. After we developed a tentative list of chapters for this book, we chose not to move immediately to outline their content. Rather, we talked about what experiences and stories were important to us in understanding each topic. Tex Sample advised us years ago to "mine your own experience." We are convinced that Taylor McConnell is right in his conviction that stories are not merely illustrations; rather stories are the foundation from which propositional truth comes. We decided to practice what we preach. The stories we tell are not included to illustrate our point. Rather, in the stories we discern meaning and life-truth.

We developed a process for collaborative writing based on trust, mutual sharing, and a willingness to "hand the disk back and forth." One of us would begin a chapter. When the disk was "handed over," the other one would revise and continue writing. The disk was handed back and forth until we were both satisfied the chapter was completed.

At first, we made a paper copy of "my" version so we could go back and retrieve what our partner changed or deleted. We soon learned that was a waste of trees. If it was so good we needed to "put it back," we should be able to remember it! There were a few times when one or the other of us would say, "You've changed that twice now. We'd better talk about it!"

One of the joys we discovered was that one of us could write until we were exhausted, or didn't have anything else to say, or didn't know where to go next. We could simply "pass the disk!" When it came back, it was different and we were able to begin again with new energy. There are no sections that are "hers" or "his." What we share with you is "ours"!

Rather than including extensive references in the text, we used only a few footnotes and included a "bibliographic essay" at the conclusion of the book. There we share with you references to the sources which enrich and inform our understanding, and our suggestions for your further exploration.

Companions who have blessed our journey include (but can never be limited to!) Taylor and June McConnell, David Fleming, SM, Carol and Paul Clark, Jim and Mary Purdy, Ellen Oliver, Joan and Bob Franklin, Joy Dillon, Lib Caldwell, Diane Olson, and our covenant group in Chicago.

We are grateful to our colleagues at Garrett-Evangelical Theological Seminary and its president, Neal Fisher, for providing us this sabbatical time. Our dean, colleague and friend, Jack Seymour, continues to support us both personally and professionally.

We give thanks to God for the Institute for Ecumenical and Cultural Research and the opportunity to be scholars in residence here. Our colleagues at the Institute have become friends, giving of themselves in many ways. We express our gratitude and thanks to them: Jon Armajani, Eugene and Dalene Botha, David Hackett, Kathleen Hughes, RSCJ; Karen and Jim Jolly; Matti and Anne Karkkainen; Delrio Ligons-Berry;

Tom Rand, OSL; and Wendy Young. Patrick Henry, Dolores Schuh, CHM; Wilfred Theisen, OSB; and Kilian McDonnell, OSB did much to create this hospitable place where we worked and worshiped with joy.

Our families are means of God's grace for us. We are aware, too, of the unnamed and unclaimed faithful whose legacy and witness penetrate our lives. For them and for you, the reader, we say, "Thanks be to God!"

Advent 1997
Institute for Ecumenical and Cultural Research
Collegeville, Minnesota

CHAPTER ONE

Falling Stars and Coloring Outside the Lines:

WONDER

Walking along the Atlantic beach on Jekyll Island early one morning in August, Linda enjoyed the feel of the smooth, white sand under her bare feet. She was hoping to find a perfect sand dollar. "I bent over and picked up a shell," she recalls. "When I discovered it was broken, I dropped it. About ten steps later, I stopped, turned, and retraced my steps. The shell I had discarded as imperfect was still there. I picked it up and laid it in the palm of my hand, running my fingers over the lovely design. God spoke to me in that moment. As I marveled at the lovely piece of that sand dollar, I came to see that it was both beautiful and partial— like my experiences of God. It didn't need to be discarded because it was broken!"

That shell is on a shelf in Linda's office and reminds us to this day of what it is—a shell, a part of the universe that once housed a sand dollar in the Atlantic—and of what it is not— whole and complete like the Truth that no one fully knows but God. *Partial* does not mean broken or no good. Partial reminds us that we are partners with others and with God—a partnership that reverberates throughout creation. On the other hand, perfectionism tempts me to claim I'm right and everyone who disagrees with me is wrong. We need to be reminded that our knowing is always partial, and others have partial truth too. We bless each other when we share—both giving and receiving—the partial truths we know.

As we walk through life, certain things and events are washed ashore. We pay particular attention to them as we walk along. Like the shell, such experiences have ongoing life in our memories. The broken sand dollar told Linda something about who she is. It uncovered meaning out of which and into which she lives. Often, the things we notice (and those we fail to notice) teach us how we are related with the world around us and what it is that provides the deep meanings out of which, and into which, we live.

Such experiences are significant for each of us. They are signs which point beyond themselves to what is meaningful (literally, filled with meaning). Some of these signs do more than point. They enable us to participate in a level of experience that is not immediately obvious. In them, the veil of ordinary experience is torn open. We are grasped from beyond. We are transformed in ways that give new meaning to life.

The word icon helps explain what we mean. Today, we may think of an icon as a computer screen graphic which allows us to enter or access a program, file, or function. Experiencing the Eastern Orthodox tradition helps us appreciate and experience the power icons can carry. At first, these icons appear to be a visual representation of Christ or the Trinity or the Holy Spirit or the saints, done in a certain style. What we have in mind is its deeper meaning. Like the computer icon, what we see is able to move us to a new place.

Icon comes from a Greek word which is usually translated *image*; it is the word used in early Greek translations of Genesis 1: "Then God said, 'Let us make humankind in our image, according to our likeness'" (Gen. 1:26). That gives us our first clue, for we assume that the words *image* and *like-*

ness do not imply that we look like God. Rather, they have to do with basic qualities of our being or our doing. The Apostle Paul used the same word when he said: "He [Jesus Christ] is the icon (translated as image) of the invisible God, the first-born of all creation; . . . He is the head of the body, the church. . . . For in him all the fullness of God was pleased to dwell, and through him God was pleased to reconcile to himself all things, whether on earth or in heaven, by making peace through the blood of his cross" (Col. 1:15, 18-20, adapted).

Note that in Jesus as icon, the "fullness of God was pleased to dwell." Jesus isn't merely a reminder of God or a picture of God, but the embodiment of God. The Eastern Orthodox tell us that an icon is a door. We are not meant to focus our attention on the doorframe. We are invited to pass through that door, to go across the threshold into a different place. An icon can be for us a door into, or a way to perceive, different dimensions of reality beyond what we initially see. Icons offer us ways to move both through and beyond the sensory and the rational. We are able to experience and comprehend relationships and growth that are both deeper and higher than our own experience would otherwise allow. For Linda, then, that partial sand dollar became an icon, opening the door to a new level of meaning.

As we look at the night sky from the deck of our mountain cabin, we sometimes see a falling star. It always surprises us. It elicts a moment of wonder and joy. For us, those falling stars point beyond themselves. They even point beyond the vastness of the universe to the God who is above and beyond and yet who cares for us. As the psalmist says,

When I look at the heavens, the work of your fingers,
the moon and the stars that you have established,
what are human beings that you are mindful of them,
mortals that you care for them?

(Psalm 8:3-4)

Dwight remembers that on his seventh birthday, the presence of a comet filled the night sky with many falling stars. They were expected, and yet each one was still a surprise. No one could predict just when or where the next one would be. You had to be looking. If you were preoccupied, you made yourself unavailable to that amazing shower of light. But for those who were ever watchful, each falling star was a unique gift.

For Linda, a "falling star" experience involved not a star but the sun. For two years she had watched her father struggle with a painful and dehumanizing journey toward death from a brain tumor. Her questioning and fist-shaking and praying left her feeling helpless and alone.

Yet, another "falling star" experience involves our son Pete. Long before the days when seat belts and car seats for small children were being used, we were driving to our campsite in the Canadian Rockies. Our preschool son, Pete, and daughter, Kris, had just been settled in the back of our VW camper to sleep. Dwight down-shifted (those old VW campers only had fifty-seven horsepower!) and our daughter said, "Pete gone! Pete bye-bye!" When Linda turned around to check on them, she screamed with fright. The back door had come open, and Pete was indeed GONE! He was nowhere in sight!

Dwight turned the van around, and we drove as quickly as we could on that curvy road. Beside the road we saw a woman with Pete in her arms. As Dwight pulled over, Linda jumped out. "Mommy, you shouldn't get out of the camper when it's moving. You might fall on your face!" Peter said.

As Linda took Peter in her arms, she saw that fiery red ball that is the sun at sunset drop behind a mountain peak. A kind of peace came over her. Somehow in that moment, she experienced that God gives life and God takes life. The gift is undeserved and full of wonder.

Because the gift of life is so good, our losses are often very painful. But God's presence and care surround us even as Linda's arms were surrounding our son (whose diagnosis after three days in the Pincher Creek Hospital was minor abrasions and multiple trauma). The gift of that moment can only be seen as God's grace bringing peace where there had been doubt, guilt, anger, and seemingly unanswerable questions.

The sand dollar on the beach was another falling star—albeit quieter and less dramatic. God sometimes graces us with peace when we are struggling for answers. God may grace us with insight when we are only seeking a shell!

Like the two disciples on the road to Emmaus, we may be so preoccupied with what we *know* that we are unable to *see*. If we continue on the journey and invite strangers to sit and share at the table with us, our eyes, too, may be opened, and we may truly know what we see!

Sometimes God's grace comes, not like a falling star, but through the eyes of a child who has resisted the restricting admonition to always "color inside the lines." Jesus reminded his hearers on more than one occasion that unless adults "change and become like children, you will never enter the kingdom of heaven" (Matt. 18:3).

Our niece, Becky, drew a picture when she was in first grade. She drew the grass with lovely blooming flowers; she left the next layer blank; and then she colored the sky blue with a brightly shining sun.

Her teacher said, "That's a nice picture, Becky, but you need to make the sky and the grass meet." Becky was adamant, "No! There is air in between." Finally the teacher, intent on convincing Becky that she was wrong and that she, the teacher, was right, called Becky over to the window. Pointing to the horizon, the teacher said, "See, Becky, the ground and the sky meet at the horizon." Unshaken, Becky said, "But I've been there and they don't!"

Like Becky's teacher, we often assume that there is only one way to look at the world. It is our way and it is the RIGHT way. When we limit truth to our way of seeing, we often fail to receive the many surprises God offers us each day. When we open our eyes, and seek to see—through the eyes of a child or from perspectives different from our own—we are often able to experience God's world (and God) in ways we never imagined. We are able to *know what we see!* We have moved beyond *seeing what we know!*

When we dare to color outside the lines, to be open to new ways of seeing and journeying, we, too, may participate in coloring wonderful pictures. We are able to see God's justice-seeking and compassion-sharing ways of being in the world.

Sometimes the lines are only in our minds—barriers that aren't even there. Our favorite example of this is to ask a group to make nine dots on paper in parallel rows of three dots.

• • •

• • •

• • •

When asked to connect all the dots by drawing four straight lines without lifting the pen from the page, most persons (who have never done this before) say it can't be done. But this is not a trick. We are unable to do this when we visualize the nine dots as a box. When we extend the lines beyond the dots, the task is simple. (See solution on page 25.)

Sometimes, our families or our cultures draw these lines. Linda was taught to "be strong" and not to give in to her emotions. Dwight learned that you should never admit your areas of vulnerability outside your own family. Both of us have had to learn to color outside those lines in order to grow in God's grace.

Some of our expectations are conditioned by our gender. If girls believe that they should never play in the mud, they may find it difficult to ever find the holy there. Yet a friend who carved a series of symbols for us included the lotus blossom because its incredible beauty can only be found growing out of mud. The beautiful pots that Richard Bresnahan creates begin with digging in the dirt and then washing it—playing in the mud. Boys may be taught (perhaps by their peers or by family) to be tough and never cry. It can be both costly and liberating when we dare to color outside some of these lines.

Seeing falling stars and coloring outside the lines lead to understanding the world and ourselves in new ways. When we say an object or event is *sign*-ificant, we recognize that it points to meaning which is not in the object or event itself. For example, we know that a red, octagonal *sign* means that we must stop. There is nothing inherent in being a red and octagonal object that involves the command to stop; but in the United States it points to that meaning, and we are expected to interpret it accordingly.

While the kind of experiences we are talking about involves pointing to meaning, something else is also happening. Symbols go beyond the meaning of signs. Something is symbolic because it involves more than an arbitrary meaning that has been assigned by the culture. A symbol participates in

19

that toward which it points. For example, a cross on a church building would function as a sign if it only told us that this building is a church. But it becomes symbol when it makes present for us the death and resurrection of Jesus Christ and God's saving grace. The best way to talk about these significant, symbolic experiences which open us to the presence of God in transforming ways is to say that they are *sacramental.* Why would we choose such a word?

For many of us the word *sacrament* is most clearly related to services of the church when we gather around a font for celebrations of the baptismal covenant or come to the Lord's Table to share in the Eucharist (also known as the Lord's Supper and Holy Communion). What happens when we gather at the Table helps us understand sacramental living.

Sometimes when we come to the Table we see only a cup, a loaf of bread, a variety of people. We sing, we pray, we listen, we share bread and the cup, we leave. We may feel uplifted or comfortable or bored or irritated. It does not take us beyond the surface level of our experiencing.

Sometimes as we receive the bread and cup, the grain and grapes remind us of our connection with the earth and with all creation. We are able to see ourselves in relation with all that God has made and is making. We feel at home in the universe.

Sometimes we look at the bread and cup and the people around us and see Jesus, the crucified and risen one, who in some mysterious way is present with us here and now. As we receive the bread and cup with the people around us, we are made aware that we are all a part of the church as the body of Christ in the world. We perceive in a different way. We see beyond what is immediately apparent. Our imagination enables us to color outside the lines, and this gives us yet another level of meaning.

And sometimes we are surprised by a level of experience even greater than these. We are grasped from beyond. We experience the vibrant presence of the transcendent God. To the eye and ear everything may seem the same, but in our souls everything is changed.

The sacramental enables us to see and receive the gift of God's presence. We know in a way beyond our senses and beyond rational proving that this great God who is above all and beyond all knowing, is also present with us in this moment. We know that God's great and unearned love for us is a sacred gift.

The sacramental was already a lived part of the Church's experience before any reflection on the sacraments took place. Until about 700 C.E. the Greek word *mysterion* and the word used to translate it into Latin, *sacramentum*, were used for a wide variety of objects and rituals.

The use of the word *mysterion* in the earliest Christian writings (including the New Testament) is an important reminder of the place of mystery in sacramental living. *Mysterion* was used in Greek religious writings long before it was appropriated by Christianity. Literally, it means closing one's mouth or lips. In the presence of the holy, a sense of awe causes us to "close our lips." We cannot adequately talk about the deepest experiences of our lives: love, beauty, or experiences of the holy. On the other hand, we cannot keep quiet about them either! A partial sand dollar can be meaning-full even though it is not complete.

Tertullian, the late-third-century North-African theologian, uses the term *sacramentum* to refer to the Trinity and to the saving work of God in history, as well as to refer to baptism and Eucharist. By translating *mysterion* (referring, for example, to the mysterious presence of God) with the Latin word *sacramentum* (one meaning of which was an oath of allegiance), we are given a hint that God's grace, human openness, and the response of faith are all components of sacramental living.

As time went on, the concept "sacrament" began to be used in a more limited way. A sacrament was to be perceived by the senses. Often the word used here was visible, but since sacraments are word/acts which can be apprehended by more than just our eyes we prefer the word *perceive* rather than visible.

Baptism involves more than the font and water and the person we see. There is the *sound* of water being poured, the *touch* in the laying on of hands, the *movement* to and from the font, and the *story* of God's continuing presence in the prayer over the water. So a sacrament came to be seen as a perceptible symbol of the sacred, both in and beyond sense perception. We call this sacred reality *grace*—God's free gift of love and care. Sacraments not only point to this grace but also become ways through which we receive this gift of God's life-transforming love.

Augustine, a fifth-century bishop in North Africa, teaches us that the sacramental involves our experiencing a holy sign—that is an image or symbol or expression of the Transcendent—through which we both perceive and receive grace. In the sacramental, a mysterious and transcendent reality comes into the world of our experience through signs/acts that we perceive with all of our senses.

These early understandings of the sacramental were based on the conviction of the Church that "God was in Christ." As the Church looked at Jesus, who had talked and slept and eaten and walked and taught and healed and expressed anger and died among them, they were aware of the presence of God in him in a unique way. In Jesus, the mystery of God's presence was embodied. As John's Gospel puts it, the "Word became flesh and lived among us, . . . full of grace and truth" (John 1:14).

Contemporary sacramental theology provides important clues for us. Jesus in his human earthly life is seen as a sacrament of the presence of God. What the disciples saw in Jesus was more than what they could see with their eyes or hear with their ears. They were convinced that Jesus embodied God's free gift of love and care in a unique way. The church continues to find in Jesus this unique embodiment of the grace of God. We too may see Jesus as sacrament.

The apostle Paul spoke of the church as the "body of Christ." Thus, the Church becomes a sacrament of the presence of Christ who is a sacrament of the grace of God. Matthew's gospel tells us: "Then Jesus told his disciples, If any want to become my followers, let them deny themselves and take up their cross and follow me" (Matt. 16:24). When we, as Christ's body, behave in self-serving and judgmental ways, we desecrate this sacrament. Persons who might have encountered God's grace through us turn away.

In addition to understanding Christ and Church as sacraments, creation may also be seen as sacramental. Creation goes beyond our immediate sense perception and not only points to God but can embody God's love and care for us in ways that transform our experience. For example, when at Eucharist we experience oneness with the universe, we may be compelled to work to heal the earth. This experience moves us to sacramental living both at the Table and in our ensuing work of healing the earth.

Our friend Bernard Cooke points to another insight: friendship is a basic human experience which is sacramental. At its deepest and best, relationships embody a reality that is above and beyond the relationship itself. In friendship, we experience the love of God. We experience the sacramental many times in our friendship as husband and wife. We experience the sacramental with close friends whose care and love and concern for us is deep. They invite us to walk with them in their good times and bad even as they walk with us through our pains and joys.

What is sacramental is characterized by paradoxes. The sacramental is both hidden and revealed, both visible and invisible, both received and perceived, both gift and response. The sacramental is embodied and present in the world we experience—it is immanent. At the same time, the sacramental opens for us the mystery of God who is beyond all our experience—it is transcendent.

What we receive, like the sand dollar Linda found, is always partial. We receive hints and clues, but the immanent transcendence of God always remains mystery as well. This sacramental revelation opens us up for what is otherwise hidden. It is hidden not because only the initiated can possess the formula for seeing what is essentially secret, but because our preoccupations blind us to the presence of the transcendent One. We continue to color inside the lines and fail to look toward the heavens.

So often, we *see what we know* instead of *knowing what we see*. We experience the sacred when we have eyes to see and ears to hear. As the writer of First John declares: "We declare to you what was from the beginning, what we have heard, what we have seen with our eyes, what we have looked at and touched with our hands, concerning the word of life" (1 John 1:1). Kathleen Hughes recently reminded us of Pierre Teilhard de Chardin's observation that nothing here below is profane for those who have eyes to see.

The sacramental is a visible and audible part of our sensible experience. We see and hear and thereby perceive hints of Christ's real presence in such significant and transforming ways that we can talk about "receiving" grace. The sacramental life seeks to be open to this invisible grace everywhere, not only in what the church calls sacraments—though most certainly there—but in all kinds of human experiences.

Some of these will be "falling stars" grasping us from beyond and surprising us—even when we are looking for them. Some will result from our learning how to be open as we let our minds "color outside the lines" and see beyond the immediately observable or the culturally acceptable. Coloring outside the lines requires that we examine and sometimes let go of many of the assumptions by which we live. Certainly, we will need to look at all our assumptions and determine if they are doorways to the sacred or roadblocks which we must remove if we are to live sacramentally.

Life's experiences have the potential for being like Linda's partial sand dollar—wonderful and significant. Sometimes these experiences may be painful. Often, for those who have the gift of seeing, they may be liberating as well. They may become for us experiences of God. But we must always remember that "we know in part," and rejoice that we have been invited into Mystery.

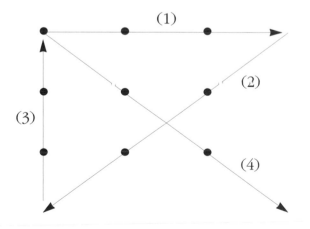

CHAPTER TWO

Sensing the Sacred:

AWE

The year Peter fell out of the van, we visited Rocky Mountain National Park before heading for the Canadian Rockies. We were excited to share the wonder and the majesty of the Rocky Mountains with our children. Peter was four at the time and always eager to experience new things.

We parked the van and headed up a trail toward a mighty waterfall. Gradually, our frustration increased as Peter dawdled along—marveling at a butterfly on the path; picking up a single piece of gravel and turning it over and over in his hand as he watched the sunlight dance over it. "Daddy, look!" he exclaimed, as he picked up a nondescript twig beside the trail.

Our initial reaction was to respond, "Do you want to see the waterfall, or not?" But suddenly we looked at one another and shook our heads! Is God to be found only in the spectacular? Through the eyes of our small child, we were brought up short. God can, indeed, be found in the wonder of a piece of gravel and a twig—if one has eyes to see!

Many of us get so caught up in the hurry and scurry of life that we fail to see God's hand at work in those seemingly insignificant, small things we encounter in our day-to-day race. Once again, we are forced to reflect on what it means to have "eyes to see" and "ears to hear." Are we so drawn to the thunder of the mighty waterfall that we fail to hear God's "still small voice" as it speaks to us over and over, every day? John Scammon, our Old Testament professor at Andover Newton Theological School, translated *still, small voice* as "the sound of a thin whisper." There may be "thin whispers" from God in surprising places, but we have to stop and look and listen, learning how to sense the sacramental.

What might we discover in that single snowflake on our daughter's cheek? What joy is to be found in the small, heart-shaped, black pebble that we found on our anniversary weekend as we walked along the shore of Lake Michigan? What is evoked within us when we see the water of our pure, ever-flowing spring catch the morning sunlight outside the kitchen window of our mountain cabin?

Our daughter, Kris, recently returned from a photography course, convinced that she will now see with new eyes the county where she and her husband Bill live. "I thought we'd looked at almost everything around here," she told us, "but we haven't begun to see it at all. We're going to go through this county road by road!" They go to a drive-in theater and observe families watching the movie on lawn chairs in the back of their pick-up trucks. They stop to photograph a farmstead with laundry flapping in the wind from a clothesline.

Sue Bender describes how an Amish quilt in a store window—meant to serve as a backdrop to sell fashionable men's tweeds—drew her in and finally served as the beginning point for the spiritual journey she chronicles in her book *Plain and Simple.* The tiny stitches that connected patches of cloth in intricate and amazing ways to create a single quilt became for her an invitation. She embarked on a journey toward a whole new way of being at home with herself and the world.

There is potential for experiencing the sacred in the everyday, taken-for-granted things that touch each of our lives. Instead of hurrying past the objects around us, sacramental living challenges us to pay attention to the *holy particular.*

This fall we are on sabbatical, living in a place different from both our home in Chicago and our mountain cabin. We decided to pack a box of items from home and cabin to help make this sabbatical apartment our *home.* It was interesting deciding what to put into that small box! We learned which things have a holy particularity for us:

- a wood sculpture carved by a dear friend and talented sculptor from the Black Hills who died much too soon;
- another by a renowned primitive sculptor from New Mexico (bought as the only remembrance of our first trip west after we were married);
- a framed photograph of our mountain cabin;
- three figures of Irish saints carved from peat and brought home from Ireland;
- and our favorite "u-no-mi" teacups (given to us by our friend and colleague Lib).

Each has significance beyond what they are. Together they spell h-o-m-e.

"Pay attention now!" Those words from a grade school teacher were a signal to us that something important was coming, something we needed to "attend to." When we begin to focus on a particular thing, we discover its unique attributes. Laura Ingalls Wilder writes about how her husband, Almanzo, ate popcorn—examining each puffed kernel with care and then eating them one at a time!

That snowflake on a cheek, that pebble on the beach, may look at first like all the others, but when we begin to really pay attention we discover their uniqueness. Whenever we pay attention to a particular kernel of corn or snowflake or pebble, we lift it out of the ordinary and mundane. It becomes something special—set apart from all others—with potential for particular meaning and value. It can become a sacrament of the ordinary.

This doesn't mean that only one pebble, one snowflake, one piece of popcorn can command our attention. Every time Dwight bakes a loaf of bread, both of us marvel at the loaf, its shape and color and texture, and above all, the smell that pervades the room. Each time a loaf of bread is baked, we experience wonder and delight; we expect that this will always be true.

No one particular loaf exists in isolation, however. As a child, Dwight would go to his grandparents' farm. Making bread was a more complicated process then than it is now with our bread machine! He remembers his Aunt Esther getting up in the middle of the night to punch down the dough so it could rise again. The aroma coming from the kitchen the next morning pulled him into that center of family and feasting with utter joy.

There is another memory too. Bread was baking in the oven when Dwight and Aunt Esther heard the cry of his uncle summoning them from the field beyond the barn. As they ran into the field, there was Grandpa lying on the stubble, having fallen from the wagon, hitting his head on the wagon tongue. Blood on the stubble, wheat ground into flour, "this is my body broken," a loaf of bread in the oven, a loaf of bread on the table in Grandma's farm kitchen, a loaf of bread on the table at our cabin, a loaf of bread on the table at Eucharist . . .

When we pay attention and open ourselves to holy particularity, we discover not only uniqueness but also connectedness. Attending to a particular object, we focus on what it evokes within us rather than describing it as it is. We pay heed because we are touched, deep inside, and change takes place—conversion, one might say. Not only is the object itself changed for us; *we* are changed by our encounter with it.

We are no longer on the outside of a thing, seeing it as an object to be used (or abused). We discover value and meaning both beyond and within that object. It remains in the world as object. Yet it addresses us in ways that make it seem like a dialogue partner in our transformation. Object becomes subject; it becomes *sign*-ificant, pointing toward something beyond its mere appearance in the world. But this value rcsides unmistakably in the particularity of the object too. Since it participates in the value and meaning which is beyond and yet within it, it becomes a symbol for us.

The loaf of bread is not just bread, although it remains something with weight and texture and color and smell, and all these are important to its uniqueness for us. It can still be used: we can eat it. But that is not all, for even in the eating, we are not primarily engaged in partaking nutritional elements. As we see, smell, touch, and taste it, something beyond it is made known to us. It becomes an epiphany—that is, a showing forth. Leonardo Boff talks about this characteristic as its "transparency." But what is transparent can almost be forgotten in the process, like the window pane you forget is there or the patio door you try to walk through. Perhaps it would be better to say it is translucent—the light shines through the object in such a way that we are aware of both the light and the object.

In one way, a pot of tea is a pot of tea, but not for us. For Dwight, tea was the adult drink that was shared with a child who was sick. It communicated warmth and love and care and returning to health. Whenever one or both of us is discouraged or upset or frustrated, the other one can be counted on to make a pot of tea. Sometimes one of us will drink a cup of tea alone, but making a pot of tea is something we do together.

So when anxiety or worry or the difficult times in our relationship come, we find ourselves making a pot of tea. More than a few times, that has been in the middle of the night. We may be having real trouble communicating with or understanding each other. One of us may have been deeply hurt and be in great pain. The pot of tea reminds us we still care deeply for each other; we extend comfort to each other through it when the words won't come. And often, as we sit together drinking tea we begin to talk, sometimes about the difficult and hard things we need to resolve. That pot of tea says that we still love each other and want the best for each other and we are in this life together.

But this sounds like a pot of tea is a medicinal comfort drink to be used only when life is filled with trouble. And nothing could be farther from the truth. We have shared pots of tea in all kinds of wonderful places that evoke rich memories: the Prince of Wales hotel in Canada with our daughter, Kris, when she was sixteen; tea and scones beside the ocean at Ballintoy, Northern Ireland; tea with milk early in the morning shared with our friend and traveling companion, Father David, in Calcutta; and a pot of tea drunk from our "unomi" cups in the sun room of our home in Chicago. There were all those mornings of "bed tea" when traveling in India and on a Caribbean cruise—a pot of tea brought to your room first thing in the morning is a wonderful way to begin the day!

When Kris and Bill were traveling with us in Ireland, they began to enjoy our tea and scone times (usually midmorning and again late afternoon). They concluded, however, that we really didn't know how to make tea! There had to be something more to it than dipping a tea bag in hot water. When we got back to the home of our friends in Belfast, Kris asked Roberta and her Mum to teach us how to make "a proper pot of tea." Now making and sharing a pot of tea is a part of our connection with friends in Ireland and Scotland and England and Canada and India and all over the United States.

The pot of tea can be what it is for us because we bring all those connections into each new experience. Each pot of tea is unique in and of itself, but it is also connected with much more. Sharing a pot of tea becomes a richly symbolic experience for us. That is always true implicitly; one doesn't have to talk about meaning each time we encounter a holy particularity for it to be there. But sometimes we do make it explicit, and we need to do that often enough to stay connected to the deeper meanings of what we are sharing.

All this has importance for our well-being as human beings and for our relationships with others; but another dimension may emerge which makes these *sign*-ificant and symbolic acts sacramental. Sharing a pot of tea becomes sacred whenever we become aware of the presence of God with us in this simple, shared act.

We believe that God is always present. Dwight had a poster in his office for many years with the words V*ocatus atque non vocatus, Deus est* (invited or uninvited, God is present). We may take that presence for granted or even be oblivious to it, but it is not continually the focus of our attention.

Sometimes we pour our cups of tea and are touched by the way nature (symbolized by the tea leaves) is poured out on our behalf. It is not only that love between us and with our friends is poured out for us, but that God comes to us, ready to be received.

Scripture invites us into these kinds of experiences. "O taste and see that the LORD is good" (Ps. 34:8). The prophet Isaiah extends God's generous invitation: "Ho, everyone who thirsts, come to the waters; and you that have no money, come, buy and eat! Come, buy wine and milk without money and without price" (Isa. 55:1).

We discover ourselves breathing in the aroma and sensing that the Holy Spirit pervades our relationship and our inmost being in mysterious ways. All these may be metaphors that contribute to the richness of our experience. At its basis however, is a simple recognition: in this pot of tea which we share, and in us who share it, God gifts us with God's presence, a source of comfort, of joy, of hope, of love.

Listening to music can be sacramental for us too, whether it be the airs of Ireland, the Brahms *Requiem* or Samuel Barber's *Adagio for Strings*. Hearing the music itself may be enjoyable. But often (and particularly with certain pieces of music), we are lifted beyond the music into the presence of the Great Composer. We resonate with the confession of Godfrey Diekmann, a Benedictine monk we first met when we were at the Ecumenical Institute twenty-five years ago and whose wit and wisdom is blessing us again this year. He observes,

> I've come to the conclusion in recent months that God is *beautiful music*; more concretely, God is *melody* . . . Is that what Clement of Alexandria had in mind when he wrote that the Word, the Logos, is not just a prose word, but the New Song; and we and all redeemed creation find the very meaning of our existence in being able to be a part of that new song.[1]

We have learned much about holy particularity from our mentors and friends, Taylor and June McConnell, who are engaged in culture-bridging work in the Santa Fe area. With their help, we have become aware of realities we would not otherwise see, or would observe only at superficial levels.

A hard-surfaced road may lead to a pueblo, but it stops before the village itself. The dirt road is an affirmation of the importance of living close to the earth. The open plaza at first appears empty. But off to a side, quite inconspicuously, one may notice some stones partially buried in the ground. There is nothing to keep one from surmising that the clearing of rocks from the area wasn't quite completed. It isn't anything that is identified with a sign or any other marker, and you won't be likely to find people talking about it to visitors. Those rocks are part of what Rina Swentzell calls the "understated sacred" in her video. We will never know what all these rocks mean to the pueblo people. It is enough to know that, for them, they are sacred, and are part of the earth that is sacred too. In their holy particularity, the rocks become translucent to the Mystery beyond. For us they become holy, too, evoking a sense of the sacred that is all around us if only we have eyes to see.

In addition to recognizing holy particularity, sacramental living sensitizes us to a sense of *sacred place.* Persons often have a particular place or space that is special—a place where we go for comfort or for quiet time with God, or just "to be" In her book *Memories of God,* Roberta C. Bondi writes of sitting in her "tall red chair across from her desk in her study." Many of us know there are special places that give us comfort—places that feel safe and protected. There are other places that cause us pain and which—even years after a bad experience—can bring on physical symptoms of fear and distress. The outdoor chapel at church camp where God seemed so close; the church where we committed our lives to one another in marriage; the cemetery where we committed the body of a loved one back to the earth and commended their soul to God—these places become *containers for grace* to which we can return and be renewed. *Place* can ground us and help us stay rooted in the important experiences of our own past and to the past that belongs to the communion of saints and our communities of faith.

Greg Eaton, a student of ours who house-sat for us one summer, named for us the importance of treating one's habitation as holy space. "Where I live needs to be an outer reflection of my soul," Greg told us. "It should be the place where I feel centered and balanced. Tending the space where I live is a purposeful, tangible way of affecting my spirituality." The two of us have approached the space in which we live with the same kind of intentionality. The arrangement of the room, what we hang on the wall and put on the tables, all are extensions of our inner selves. Our space both affirms and generates our sense of the sacramental.

Kathleen Norris became so attuned to place that she entitled a book *Dakota: A Spiritual Geography.* She reminds us that the stories of desert hermit monks and Celtic monastics are filled with "monks in love with a place." Her experiences on the plains of South Dakota speak to us, and sometimes for us, as we journey with her across those plains to what is sacred space for us.

Soon after we began teaching at Westmar College in Le Mars, Iowa, in the mid-sixties, we took a vacation trip with our three children. Our goal was the Rocky Mountains, but we had never been to the Black Hills. We thought we really ought to stop to see Mount Rushmore. We settled into a campsite in Wind Cave National Park for three nights and began to explore the area. What a surprise to discover that these "hills" are mountains. As we drove the back roads and hiked the trails, we were captivated by the ways in which this beauty is so accessible—not remote, majestic, and austere, but inviting and hospitable. We went to Mount Rushmore and were impressed with the gigantic sculpture of "the faces" (as they are known in the area). But even more, we delighted in the gentle winding walkway making its way past trees and bushes and great out-croppings of rock. Even the buildings seemed to grow out of the mountain, their low lines merging into the natural beauty of that place. Our three-day visit stretched into ten days. We knew when we left we would return again and again. And we have, every summer for thirty years except the year Linda was completing her doctorate.

A few years later we found nearly four acres of forest, mountainside, and high meadow for sale. We started camping there the day we signed the papers, and we felt connected to this place from the beginning. We call it *The Birds' Nest* (*Vogel* is the German word for bird). Its rocks and trees and flowers, the flowing spring, the sound of the stream just across the road, the call of the birds, the mountain peaks around us—all make it sacred space. We are not the first to feel this way; the native peoples of this land knew it was holy long before Europeans arrived.

We have become increasingly impressed with the ways our own spiritual journey is connected to and, indeed, affected by *place*. Linda has a hammock, hung between two towering ponderosa pines behind our cabin at The Birds' Nest. Lying in it, looking up at puffy, white clouds moving across the deep blue sky and watching the pine boughs sway in the wind, she often feels a deep connection with God. Her connection with God in these mountains which were known as *Paha Sapa* to the native peoples who hunted and worshiped here long ago, sweeps beyond time and culture.

The 1970s were a time of confrontations between Native American descendants and some Euro-Americans who now live in this place. We heard someone assert that "the Indians lost their right to these Black Hills. They had it for hundreds of years and never timbered them or mined them. If you don't use it, you lose it!" What a telling judgment on modern, Euro-American culture! Part of what draws us to this land is the legacy of the importance of living in harmony with the earth, knowing that it is sacred. This understanding is essential for sacramental living. If we hope to continue to live on a planet that can sustain and support life, our nation and global community must recapture this perspective.

The very first thing Linda does each morning at our cabin is to go out on the front deck and exclaim, "Good morning, Morning!" It has become a prayer of thanksgiving. And the last thing she hopes to do each night is to turn out all of the lights, go out into the cool (cold!) night air where no human light shines, gaze up at the North Star and the Milky Way, and whisper, "Good night, Night!" In fact, going out into the darkness to look at the heavens which seem so close to us is a nightly ritual we delight to share with our guests. Close friends Joan and Bob wrote to us indicating that for them, looking at the night sky from The Birds' Nest marks the standard by which all other stargazing is measured!

As we reflect on our own spiritual geography, we are able to identify those places which help to keep us connected with God and with our family roots. As we reflect on our own spiritual journey, we find places to which we need to return, where God touches and teaches us.

Richard Foster reminds us that the paths we take do not produce the change; our paths only "put us in the place where change can happen." Being quietly attentive to the places where we find ourselves, simply being present to where we are and what surrounds us will open us up to what it is God would have us be and know. Returning to those special places and taking time to absorb what they have to give, invigorates us and helps keep us centered.

Our friend Paul needs to return to Ely, Minnesota, each summer—if only for a few days. His wife, Carol, goes with him to Ely and he goes with her to Sanibel Island—a place where she feels most connected and finds renewal. There are other places they love to go (and sometimes we go with them). We share memories of sitting on the porch of the Hillside Hotel in Door County, Wisconsin, and watching the water of Ephraim Bay lap the shore; they come to Chicago and we visit museums and walk along the beach by Lake Michigan. We experience God's presence in these places too. But there is often for each person one special place where we know we truly need to go if we are to remain connected and grow toward wholeness.

Carol Rutledge shares her diary during the time she was living in Topeka, Kansas. Her mother was dying one hundred miles away—through the Flint Hills of the Kansas prairie—in Hope, Kansas. Readers are invited to journey with her—both geographically and spiritually. Because Linda grew up in Topeka, Dwight in a town near Hope, and we both lived in Kansas until we were married, we journeyed along with her. She drew us back home to dramatic changes in the weather, wind that will not quit, waving grass that looks purple at sunset, a sky so wide that you believe it has no end.

Carol's diary drew us both back to Kansas and our own hurried trips to the bedsides of dying parents. We know the sense of helplessness when others are trying to save a life that is valiantly trying to say "good-bye" and die. We, too, know the pain of knowing there is nothing more we can do.

We have heard it said, "Why would anyone ever choose to

drive across the Kansas prairie?" "It's so flat (not true)! It's miles and miles of nothing but miles and miles!" But for those who will open themselves to the world we grew up in, there is much to be learned from allowing oneself to become attuned to the prairie. And if this can be true here (those who do not know what it is to love the prairie will say), it can be true anywhere.

Some who grow up on the prairie say they feel hemmed in and oppressed in a forested terrain. Others who have grown up in less open landscapes sometimes feel naked and exposed when they can see for miles and miles and there is seemingly no place to find refuge. We have discovered that God speaks to us both in the forests and on the prairie if we open ourselves to the messages that each may offer. We believe that God speaks everywhere and always if we will only "tune in" and "attend." As the psalmist asserts:

> Where can I go from your spirit?
>> Or where can I flee from your presence?
> If I ascend to heaven, you are there;
>> if I make my bed in Sheol, you are there.
> If I take the wings of the morning
>> and settle at the farthest limits of the sea,
> even there your hand shall lead me,
>> and your right hand shall hold me fast.
>>>> (Psalm 139:7-10)

Terry Williams works as a volunteer with the educational program of a museum in Salt Lake City. She admits to believing that museum education is meant to be about the business of "waking people up to their surroundings." There is no more appropriate spiritual task for persons from many different faith traditions than being in touch with the land and water and sea and air—with all that makes up our universe and beyond.

Planting our roots, being connected with our own place and space, and being attuned to others' place and space are spiritual disciplines which foster sacramental living.

Native Americans teach us that no one can own what God has created. We are stewards of what we have been given or what we have taken (and we need to seek to be responsible for what our ancestors have done). To live in harmony with creation is a part of what it means to claim citizenship in the global village. Tilden Edwards calls our everyday, plain living in the places where we find ourselves "the path of naked, simple faith." This path holds for us grace and hope, challenges and disappointments, and the assurance that God walks this path and is in these places with us.

We are helped to recognize God's presence in those special places where we both perceive and receive the presence of God. When we stand high on a cliff above waves crashing on the rocks below, we become aware of the awesome power of God. This power carves out great bays and washes away high and mighty cliffs. It reminds us that it is a delusion to believe that we are ever in control.

When we stood at the top of Little Devil's Tower in South Dakota and saw what appeared to be a huge orange log, we were astonished to discover thousands of ladybugs. God has such a wonderful and amazing plan for these tiny creatures. Surely, God's plan for all of us is equally wondrous if we will only stay attuned!

Our friend Brent Sturm described for us a powerful and life-changing experience. He volunteered to be a guide when the Project NAMES AIDS Memorial Quilt was spread out between the steps of the Capital and the Washington Monument covering the entire Mall. He had responsibility for five hundred panels of the quilt. He was privileged to share with thousands of people who came including family members and friends and lovers of those persons memorialized by the panels in his section. He wrote about his experiences in *Sacramental Life*: "I removed only three pieces of litter from those five hundred panels the entire weekend: a film canister, a tissue, and a wire twist tie. People understand holy ground!"

When we—like Brent Sturm, Terry Williams and Carol Rutledge—find ourselves coming face to face with dying and grief, we can learn and find great comfort in the world which surrounds us. The flint hills of Kansas, the Great Salt Lake Basin with its fluctuating lake level that ebbs and flows into and out of sanctuaries for birds and other wild life, and the Mall in Washington, District of Columbia, can all be places to meet and be held by God.

Linda's stepfather was deeply loved by both of us and by our children. When we shared the Black Hills with him, he fell in love with them even as Linda's mother had years earlier. He wanted to have his ashes scattered in those mountains. The summer after his unexpected and sudden death, we found ourselves in a clearing on a mountainside, singing songs, reading poems and scripture, scattering ashes to help nourish the beautiful wild flowers. Harney Peak seemed to touch the sky as we looked toward it. That sacred space, already holy, is further blessed by our memory of his life and love.

There may be a danger in our focusing on the world of nature, as if God were present only in natural beauty. Great cities, too, are places where God is. We remember, more than thirty years ago, hearing Malcolm Boyd (Episcopal priest and poet) say, "They asked me how I dared to take Jesus into that gay bar. I told them, 'Oh, I'm not taking Jesus there—I'm meeting him there!'"

Linda and I grew up on the Kansas prairie and taught and ministered for twenty-five years in Iowa. We found God in the sacred spaces of both places as well as in the Paha Sapa—the beautiful Black Hills. For the past ten years, we've lived in the city of Chicago. Some of our friends from past years are surprised to discover that we love that great city. As we drive on Lake Shore Drive, never ceasing to marvel at the skyline at night, we turn to each other and say, "Can you believe it? This is our home town!"

One of our favorite places is the chapel in the sky at the Chicago Temple (First United Methodist Church of Chicago). There, on the front of the Lord's Table, is carved a scene of Christ weeping over the city of Chicago—reminiscent of Christ weeping over Jerusalem. Christ weeps over our cities and over our raped countryside. But Christ also rejoices wherever someone finds the Christ in "one of the least of these" and offers nurture and hospitality.

We have said that Christ is a sacrament of the presence of God. That is true, not only for shepherd fields outside Bethlehem or the shores of the Sea of Galilee. It is true also of the busy streets of Jerusalem . . . and Chicago. God is present not only in moments of joy and delight in the natural world. God is also present in the lives of each one who inhabits with us this sacred space we call the earth.

Sacred space is not an unreal idealized setting where everything is right. Jerome Theisen, abbot at Saint John's from 1979 to 1992 when he was elected Abbot Primate of all Benedictines, knew that about holy space:

> Saint John's is a place of struggle and mystery. It is
> a struggle for the monks to come to some realiza-
> tion of who they are as human beings, Christian

believers, and monastic persons. Saint John's is a place of trial, discernment, and decision. . . . Saint John's is not utopia (no place). It is some place. It is not the kingdom to come; it is not a perfect community. It is not a place without problems, nor a people without problems. But it is a place to seek God. It is a place where one is constrained to seek God.[2]

Sacred space can be desecrated. The church where we were married was demolished to make room for an expressway. The beautiful red Queen Anne home with white trim in which we lived for twenty years and nurtured our family was bulldozed to make way for a duplex whose main feature seems to be a wide driveway and four garage doors where plants and trees and lawn used to be. And those national monument buildings that blended into the natural beauty around Mount Rushmore are no more. Instead there is a hulking parking garage, a great entrance made of imported stone which dwarfs the sculpture above, and a wide thoroughfare that would be more in keeping with a monument in Washington, District of Columbia, than in the Black Hills. The open pit mines scarring the earth in the northern hills also testify to the desecration of sacred space. But we have gradually learned that, by God's grace, nature keeps reclaiming what is taken from her and that alternative sacred spaces can be found.

We climbed the long ladder leading to the Anasazi (Navajo word meaning *ancient ones*) cliff dwellings high above the mesa in northern New Mexico at Bandelier National Monument. It was January and there was snow and quiet all around. We were with a group of students who were participating in a cross-cultural seminar. Taylor and June McConnell were the seminar leaders. Taylor told us of a previous visit when one of the students was an Ojibway from Wisconsin who was studying for the ministry at a seminary in the east. He brought his flute along when his group made this climb. June sat under a stately pine near the bottom of the ladder because she had had a hip replaced, and the climb up the long, steep ladder was too risky for her. As the students sat quietly around the kiva high up in this cliff dwelling of long ago, the Ojibway student began to play his flute.

The group suddenly saw a great eagle circling in the sky above. Its grace and grandeur held the group spellbound. Gently it landed high above June on a branch of the pine tree. It was a spine-tingling experience. There was nothing to do but sit in awe and absorb the thousands of years of history that had been lived in that place and recognize that the God who was worshiped at this sacred kiva long ago continues to watch over those who come to this day. Later, as the students were marveling at their good fortune in the timely visit of the eagle, the Native American student said softly, "I called him in with my flute."

As our seminar group sat there that day, we were deeply moved by the recounting of this story of grace that connected us with others (both recent and ancient) and with this place. We felt the quiet presence of One who is Mystery and who we know as the God of Abraham and Sarah (also *ancient ones*) and of those who follow in The Way. The cliff dwellings high above the ruins of ancient dwellings on the mesa, the kiva where people worshiped thousands of years ago, the whiteness of the snow, the gentle whisper of the wind in the pines, and the blue of the sky above made us aware of the presence of God—God with us, God with all who have walked and will walk this earth.

Wherever there is pain, wherever there is lack of meaning, wherever there is hopelessness—there is God, waiting for us to join in the bringing of hope where there is none, and the bringing of the *kin-dom* of God to our hurting and hurt-ful world. There is no *place* where God is not! But unless we are able to sense the sacramental, we will, too often, be unaware of that presence.

We began this chapter inviting you to think with us about *particular things* and *special places* that can be sacramental for us, translucent windows of the sacred. We end it by suggesting that God is to be seen in, and offers us grace through, every thing and in all places—if we have eyes to see and ears to hear.

Notes

1. Kathleen Hughes, *The Monk's Tale: A Biography of Godfrey Diekmann* (Collegeville, Minn: The Liturgical Press, 1991), 314.

2. *A Sense of Place II: The Benedictines of Collegeville*, ed. Colman J. Barry, O.S.B. (Collegeville, Minn: The Liturgical Press, 1990), 17. (This book is a fascinating collection of observations from monks at Saint John's Abbey.).

CHAPTER THREE

Kindling the Fire:

STORIES & RITUALS

The first day of our first visit to Ireland was filled with wonder. We marveled at the tomb at Newgrange, constructed more than five thousand years ago with its stone-corbeled roof that still does not leak. We wandered among the ruins of the twelfth-century Cistercian abbey at Mellifont and gazed at the intricate carvings on the high crosses at Monasterboice. As dusk fell, we made our way back toward our bed-and-breakfast lodging. At one intersection, a small sign pointed to a side road to the Hill of Slane. Perhaps prompted by the Spirit, we turned up that road.

There were no other cars at the small car park. We walked through the gate and up the hill, past the crumbling walls of the monastery and the ancient shell of a church. As the evening shadows gathered around us, we looked across the valley of the Boyne River to the hill of Tara, home of the high kings of Ireland. It was a peaceful moment, with no sounds but the song of a bird. The relics of the past and the beauty of the Irish countryside combined to evoke a sense of awe.

However, it was the story we found in the guidebook that made the experience sacramental for us. Centuries before, Saint Patrick (385-461 C.E.) had come to the top of the Hill of Slane on Easter eve. At Tara, ten miles across the valley, the

Druid festival of Beltane was about to be celebrated. All fires, inside and out, were to be extinguished. The Druids would light a large ceremonial fire at Tara from which all other fires were to be lit.

On the Hill of Slane with darkness all around, Patrick kindled a large fire for the Easter vigil. The high king and the Druid priests at Tara must have been astonished as they looked across the valley to Slane. Such a brazen act was considered illegal and blasphemous, punishable by death. As those at Tara watched in surprise, horror, and anger at such an affront to their beliefs, tradition has a Druid priest telling the king: "If that fire isn't put out tonight, it will burn forever." It was not put out. Patrick appeared before the court on Easter morning to give his witness, and the light that testifies to Christ's resurrection continues to shine forth in Ireland, even in the midst of "the Troubles."

We weren't on the Hill of Slane with Patrick; we aren't even Irish by family heritage. But that story has entered our lives, changing us by the transforming power it carries. It calls us to kindle our own fires—fires that may be a threat to the culture in which we live!

After we returned home from our visit to that quiet hillside, we discovered that the hymn tune to which we sing "Be Thou My Vision" is called Slane. The peat-sculpted figure of Saint Patrick we brought with us to Collegeville shows him standing beside the paschal fire he kindled on the hill of Slane that Easter eve. The courageous action of Patrick was itself a living out of the death and resurrection theme of Easter—and of baptism.

Does that mean that stories only illustrate truths and embody teachings? We regularly use stories to illustrate the point. But where did the point come from? Often the point comes from a story in the first place! Stories have power far beyond their ability to serve as examples. Our moralizing at the end of a story often gets in the way more than it illuminates. Stories have power to speak God's truth to all who have ears to hear!

When we said that Patrick's action embodies the theme of death and resurrection central to Easter and to baptism, we did not stop to think where that theme came from. On reflection, we know that both Easter and baptism are based on the *story* of Christ's life, death, and resurrection. In fact, the preaching of the early church as we find it in the Acts of the Apostles is the telling of that story over and over again. When our theological affirmations or spiritual truths lose contact with the story, we are deprived of the deep evoking of meaning that the narrative carries.

Easter services usually tell the story of the Resurrection, but it is at the Easter Vigil that the full sweep of salvation history is presented to us most fully. Neither of us had ever been to an Easter Vigil until we were in Collegeville with the Benedictines twenty-five years ago. Since then the Easter Vigil has become our favorite service of the church year, as most of our students and parishioners over the last quarter-century know full well!

Early in the service, an extensive number of readings from the Bible tell the story of salvation history beginning with the Creation and concluding with the Resurrection. At no other time in our services of worship do we hear the sweep of God's saving acts presented in such broad strokes.

The mighty acts of God beginning with creation are proclaimed in Word and song. We remember the great flood and God's covenant to Noah with the giving of the rainbow. Abraham and Sarah's decision to follow God's call and journey in faith is recalled. Then we are reminded that, although God is always faithful and keeps promises, the people rebelled and finally found themselves as slaves in Egypt. We rejoice with Moses and Miriam as they led the people out of bondage into freedom. We hear the prophet Isaiah's call to all people—poor and rich—to return to God and find there the abundant life. Jeremiah assures God's people, at a time when their unfaithfulness had led them into catastrophic circumstances yet again, that God will renew them and replace their hearts of stone with new hearts. We are invited to see with Ezekiel all those lifeless dry bones that will be raised to life in God by the inbreathing of the Spirit.

This continuing story, then, we claim as our own as we witness to the death, burial, and resurrection of Jesus Christ. In the baptismal covenant we celebrate during our Easter Vigil, we come to know in powerful ways that we too can die to self and be made new persons. We can have a new heart on which is written the love and saving grace of God.

In some churches, this sweeping story is not told at Easter. But the account of the Resurrection apart from this larger story is greatly impoverished. Too often, baptisms are brief rites with little reference to the story. But when and where the prayer of thanksgiving over the water is prayed, the story of God's dealing with us through the symbol of water is rehearsed in a way which can evoke deep meaning:

> When nothing existed but chaos,
>   you swept across the dark waters
>   and brought forth light.
> In the days of Noah
>   you saved those on the ark through water.
> After the flood you set in the clouds a rainbow.
> When you saw your people as slaves in Egypt,
>   you led them to freedom through the sea.
> Their children you brought through the Jordan
>   to the land which you promised. . . .

In the fullness of time you sent Jesus,
nurtured in the water of a womb.
He was baptized by John and anointed by your Spirit.
He called his disciples
    to share in the baptism of his death and resurrection
    and to make disciples of all nations.[1]

And those brief references call to mind the fuller form of the stories we have read and heard.

It is not so much that stories illustrate doctrines, Taylor McConnell observes, as that doctrine is the skeleton of the story! We may usc stories to point to a spiritual truth. But at their most potent, the story invites us in, and we are able to participate in the relationship with God it evokes. We become a part of the story; it becomes a part of us, and we are changed.

In her teaching, Linda maintains that we miss a powerful opportunity with the children and youth in our confirmation classes when we begin by teaching the Apostles' Creed or doctrinal affirmations. These evolved from the church's hammering out orthodox answers to questions which may have been forgotten or, at the very least, may not be *our* questions. Sharing our faith might be more faithfully and effectively done by inviting our students into the stories of Jesus as he interacted with all kinds of folks.

In fact, the literal meaning of the word *orthodox* centers not on right beliefs but in *right praise*. The Apostles' Creed was originally in the form of questions: "Do you believe in God the Father? Do you believe in Jesus Christ? Do you believe in the Holy Spirit?" And the answer was a ringing "Credo!" Often *credo* is translated "I believe," but the root meaning is "I set my heart upon." Our answer means "I stake my life on this!"

What we too often communicate is the importance of believing that certain affirmations are true. When we pause and look at the language, we notice that in the creed we say, "I believe *in* God the Father, *in* Jesus Christ, *in* the Holy Spirit" (italics ours). When we believe *in* (that is, when we put our trust in) someone, there is likely to be a story involved—either a story on the basis of which we trust, or a story about what happened when we did trust. It is out of the stories of living relationships that sacramental living comes. When we come to know Jesus as our brother, our friend, and our savior we are empowered to "set our hearts" and "stake our lives" on him by saying "yes" to the gift of God's saving grace. We become a part of Christ's body, the Church.

The stories of God's people preserved in the Old and New Testaments teach us who and Whose we are. Other powerful stories throughout history (such as Patrick on the Hill of Slane) also teach us what it means to be a follower of Jesus. Our own life stories and the stories of our communities of faith serve as icons that help to shape our ways of being and doing.

When we were looking for a congregation to be our church home in the city of Chicago, we made up a short list of United Methodist congregations to visit. First, we went to worship at Epworth United Methodist Church. We never made it to any others on the list! Epworth knows who and Whose it is, and the persons in that community are quick to share their stories. Through those stories we learned what it means to be a part of Epworth.

Epworth was once an affluent congregation near Lake Michigan on the north side of the city. But times change, and the North Shore came to mean suburbs like Wilmette and Winnetka. Ethnic peoples moved in; apartments were subdivided; the neighborhood changed. The congregation found itself "huddled in its lovely little chapel" with a pastor who said, "We'll just have to let the sanctuary roof leak. We're going to die anyway!"

Then a newly retired pastor, Bill White, whose father had served the congregation when it was vital and growing, was asked to become interim pastor at Epworth. He accepted the invitation. And he said to the people huddled in their chapel: "If we want to live, we have to open the front doors to the neighborhood." And that is what they decided to do.

One morning, several older women who had been working at the church decided to go to a nearby café for lunch. When they got there, everyone was talking about the man who had frozen to death in the dumpster in the alley behind the church the night before. They came back to the church determined that no one else would freeze to death while they had a gym that could be used as a shelter for the homeless.

It is not easy to deal with neighbors, bureaucrats, and politicians in the city of Chicago, but Epworth perseveres. At the beginning, members (including women and men beyond seventy years of age) stayed all night to supervise what is now a center where up to sixty-five men are able to find hospitality, safety, a mattress with clean bedding, and warmth. Our shelter is open from November through April each year and is an integral part of who we understand ourselves to be as the people of God in our part of Chicago.

The church's tutoring program serves more than 125 children from preschool through high school. We are ethnically diverse with almost equal thirds of our congregation being African and African American, Filipino American, and European American. We are a reconciling congregation—

openly welcoming to gays, lesbians, and bisexual persons. We like to think that we are openly welcoming to everyone; we often have homeless persons and mentally challenged persons worshiping with us.

Our prayer time each Sunday morning reflects who we are as a congregation. During our time of joys and concerns, Larry shares that he has been elected president of his sixth grade class; his mother says had it not been for his tutor, Roger, and our tutoring program, he could never have written and given his campaign speech. Eleanor asks us to continue remembering in our prayers her neighbor who is struggling with alcoholism. Beth tells us the youth choir is going to take the "el" downtown to participate in a hunger walk and asks for our prayers. Jim raises concerns about turmoil and conflict in a particular country of Africa or in Northern Ireland. A young couple shares with us that they are going to have a baby. A child asks us to pray for a classmate who was shot last week. On and on it goes (our service never ends in an hour). We are moved to laughter and to tears. The story of Epworth is the story of the intersection of these concerns lifted up in the presence of our brothers and sisters and of God, whom we know through Jesus Christ.

Persons who come to visit quickly learn that we care about one another and our world. Although we had only been attending for a few weeks, the congregation wrapped us in care when Dwight's parents died in Kansas within three weeks of each other.

Dwight's father was frail and in poor health, so it was not a great surprise when the call came to tell us he had gone into a coma. When we arrived late that evening, a friend of the family told us, "He's still alive, just barely. I think he's waiting for you." We went in to be with Mother at his bedside. We prayed with Dad. We proclaimed Psalm 121 together. Dwight prayed, "Lord, now let your servant depart in peace, according to your word, for my eyes have seen your salvation" (The *Canticle of Simeon*).[2] Later when Dwight had taken Mother back to her apartment, Linda began to sing the words of Natalie Sleeth's song: "Go now in peace, go now in peace, . . ." And with those words, she sang him over. It seemed those words gave him permission to let go and accept God's gift of peace.

There is a story within this story, however. Psalm 121 was not just a favorite psalm of Dad's, although it was that. He had been the first person from his rural community in Missouri to go to college and to graduate from seminary. His first appointment was as pastor of a church in Ponca City, Oklahoma. It was a long way from his farm home east of St. Joseph, Missouri. He didn't know anyone in Ponca City. He didn't know anyone anywhere near Ponca City. He was single; he would be going alone, a stranger in a strange land.

Dwight's grandmother gathered the family in their farmhouse living room just before he left and read Psalm 121:

I lift up my eyes to the hills—
from where will my help come?
My help comes from the LORD,
who made heaven and earth.
He will not let your foot be moved,
he who keeps you will not slumber.
He who keeps Israel
will neither slumber nor sleep.
The LORD is your keeper;
the LORD is your shade on your right hand.
The sun shall not strike you by day,
nor the moon by night.
The LORD will keep you from all evil;
he will keep your life.
The LORD will keep

your going out and your coming in,
from this time forth and forevermore.

All through his growing years, Dwight remembers that when it was time to leave his grandmother's bedside, the family would gather to read Psalm 121. His father read it in their living room when Dwight was leaving for college. They read it when we left Kansas as a newly married couple to go all the way to the big city of Boston for graduate school. We read it at the end of every visit as we left Dwight's parents' home. We read it when our eldest son Mark left for the United States Air Force and when our daughter left for college. It marked all our times of parting. It was natural, then, for us to turn to those words as an assurance to Dwight's dad as he faced death.

Reading Psalm 121 is more than the words, important as they are. That particular pattern of words is a sign pointing to the family story, and the family story is a symbol of God's promise to be with us. Even more, the story is one we live within, certain that God's love and care enfold us come what may. It is a path of sacramental living prepared for us by our family's experience.

Why can stories evoke such a deep sense of connection for us? Compare the way in which we respond to the previous paragraph with one of the stories we shared with you earlier. The sentences in the last paragraph may help clarify what we are trying to say. By focusing on certain facets of the story, we limit the scope of our attention. We sculpt meaning out of our family's experience with Psalm 121 by isolating certain aspects of it, describing them as clearly and coherently as we can.

Such a process is helpful (at least, we hope it is). But it comes at a cost. In order to focus, we set boundaries to our attention. We can make certain observations only by not attending to others. The experience is thus circumscribed by the process of intellectual reflection that helps us attend to certain kinds of meaning.

A story, on the other hand, does not have sharp boundaries. It addresses the whole person: our thinking, our remembering, our feeling, and our hoping. When stories really speak to us, they evoke a response in our inmost being. We enter the story; we are grasped by it so that it is no longer something outside us. We become participants in its narrative. A fire is kindled within us.

In 1985, we were appointed pastor and minister of education at St. Luke's United Methodist Church in Dubuque, the oldest congregation in Iowa. The first time we entered that lovely building, we discovered carved on the arch above the chancel these words from Psalm 121: *"He that Keepeth Israel Shall neither Slumber nor Sleep."* When we saw it, we knew we were home!

We receive a story. When it is sacramental, it becomes translucent. When we read about Patrick on the Hill of Slane, we become aware that this story is not just about something that happened to a man we never met, on a hill we had not visited before, in the far-distant past. Our sense of being is addressed; through that story we perceive a reality that transcends both the facts of the story and our individual lives. We are incorporated into another reality and transformed by it.

Being incorporated and transformed is what can happen when we come to the Lord's Table to share in the Eucharist. At its very foundation, this great feast of the Church is based on a story. In Corinthians, Paul says, as it were, "Let me tell you a story, a true story that was told to me, how our Lord Jesus, on the night when he was betrayed, took bread, and when he had given thanks . . ." (1 Cor. 11:23-24, AP).

But we miss the whole point if we think that our feast is about something that happened only in the past. It is also a present action. Something happens to us here and now. We become a part of the story. It grasps us. It is not just about Jesus back then; it is also about us now.

It connects us to other stories as well. There is the Passover meal before Moses led the Israelite slaves out of Egypt and all the Passover meals that have been celebrated by Jews around the world from that time to this present day. We remember Jesus eating with Zacchaeus (the tax collector he found peering down at him from a sycamore tree); Jesus eating with Mary, Martha and Lazarus; Jesus feeding the five thousand; Jesus sharing his last supper with his disciples in that upper room. We remember the resurrected Christ breaking bread with the two disciples with whom he had walked on the road to Emmaus. We remember Jesus sharing fish with his disciples at that early morning breakfast on the shore.

These stories are interwoven with many Eucharist meals we have shared:

- at our wedding,
- at the funeral of a loved one or dear friend,
- with Marianist brothers and priests in Bangalore, India,
- with that diverse and caring group of brothers and sisters in Christ who kneel with us at the communion rail at Epworth,
- at Easter Vigils at St. Luke's,
- with the sisters of St. Benedict in the chapel of the Sacred Heart,
- at countless memorable celebrations of Eucharist in the Chapel of the Unnamed Faithful at Garrett-Evangelical with students and colleagues,
- and at the small informal eucharist celebrations in Howe's chapel.

"This bread which we break, is it not a sharing in the body of Christ?" And to make clear what is happening, when Dwight presides he usually adds: "whose body *we* are." For Paul makes it clear: we are the body of Christ, and when we share the broken bread, we are united to one another. As Augustine taught us, "It is your own mystery you receive."

Mystery, indeed! A story never pretends to contain everything. Each eucharistic experience hints at what came before and what might come after; it assumes that other stories are going on around it. Realities are carried within and beyond it. Yet, Eucharist can be an icon through which we are transported into a realm of deep meaning and in which the transcendent God becomes Emmanuel—*God with us.*

Whenever our celebrations of Eucharist are removed from stories—both past and present—which fill them full of meaning, they are in danger of becoming dead rituals which lack power and saving grace. On the other hand, rituals that grow out of stories we know and claim as our own can enrich and transform our lives.

Ritual acts that are most meaningful are usually connected to stories that hold truth for us. Sometimes we don't even realize that we have created a ritual until after the fact. Sometimes rituals birth stories.

When our children were young, we struggled to find ways to keep Advent as a time for preparing for the celebration of Christmas. But we loved to decorate our home and experience a sense of festivity with college students before they left to go home for Christmas. For us, Advent is a time of joyous expectation, rather than penitential solemnity. So every year we decorated our home the Saturday before the first Sunday in Advent. We put the stable from our crèche in a prominent place in our dining room. Only an empty manger, the cow, and some sheep were in it. The magi were far away in an east window in our library. Mary and Joseph and their donkey started out on a table in the living room. The shepherds were out in a field with their sheep, gathered around a fire circle, made with driveway gravel and toothpick logs. Gradually during Advent, Mary and Joseph moved closer to the stable. On Christmas Eve they arrived. Then, during the twelve days of Christmas, the magi made their journey from the east arriving on Epiphany, January 6.

After our daughter Kris was grown, we asked her, "What is Christmas for you?" "That's easy," she said, "it's when we come home from church on Christmas Eve and put the baby Jesus in the manger and hang the angel above him!" For Kris, the story of Christmas, the meaning of Christmas, is wrapped up in our simple family ritual. Year after year, wherever we are on Christmas Eve, we take the empty manger away and replace it with the manger with the baby in it. We hang our ceramic angel on the nail at the peak of our stable's roof.

We bought our crèche figures at a dime store in Quincy, Massachusetts, as we prepared to celebrate our first Christmas as a new family in 1959. When Kris was sixteen, we were traveling in Europe together. We said, "Wouldn't it be neat to buy a new crèche set here in Italy?" Kris was incensed! "Get rid of our crèche! Why?" That was one "neat idea" that was laid to rest almost before it was uttered! We suspect that when we no longer need a crèche set, Kris's family will become the proud owners of an "antique crèche set" from Woolworth's (complete with gravel and toothpicks)!

What is a ritual anyway? It has something to do with a *repeated pattern*; a ritual is something we do over and over again, in much the same way. This repeated pattern *points to a meaning that is greater than the action itself.* We see elements of ritual in the way Linda greets each morning at our cabin and in our making and drinking a pot of tea. Many of our repeated acts are latent rituals.

We know that in Japanese culture, the tea ceremony is a highly developed ritual, with its own meaning, both richer and deeper than ours. Ours takes on additional meaning for us because we have shared in Japanese tea ceremonies. Lighting candles on our table before we eat is not the same as the mother of a Jewish family lighting candles each Sabbath evening. But our act that is a latent ritual is enriched because we make this connection with an ancient and living Jewish ritual.

One of our graduate students and a good friend told Linda recently about an important family ritual. Dori and Lincoln Baker and their daughter, Erin, have developed the habit of taking a detour by the lagoon on the Northwestern University campus on their way home after Sunday morning worship. They bring bread to feed the carp.

Then their family was devastated by the stillborn birth of Sophia—who had been greatly anticipated and was already much loved. The following Sunday, their family did what they always do—they walked to the lagoon before going home. Having been fed at church, they stopped to feed the fish. Being fed, connecting worship and feeding the fish, strengthening family ties when grief tears at our hearts—this simple family ritual, so familiar, so ordinary, holds them steady when their world is torn apart.

We need words to describe these *sign*-ificant repeated patterns we call rituals and to clarify their meaning. Even before there are words, there are *gestures*—bodily actions and reactions that are our earliest and most fundamental way of experiencing. When a baby cries, experiences the love and security of being held and rocked, and responds to that action by snuggling close to our heart, the basis for significant relationship is established. Being held points to and participates in the relationship of parent and child. Whether or not we want to use the word *symbolic* to refer to such a prelinguistic experience, it is important to remember that life is more than words.

Andy Smith, beloved pastor of Custer Community Church (our home congregation whenever we are at our cabin), encouraged the congregation there to hold hands even across the aisles and from row to row while singing the benediction response:

Grant us thy peace upon our homeward way;

With thee began, with thee shall end the day . . .[3]

Pastors have come and gone since Andy's days in Custer. But, without a word of direction from the worship leader or from the bulletin, the congregation just keeps on holding hands. They reach out to the many visitors and tourists who find their way to worship in that place. Without a word, all those present become a part of this binding act.

This act of holding hands is something they "do by heart." Gabe Huck teaches us that doing something by heart means more than just doing it by memory; it is something that speaks to and for us. It is a bodily experience, and for some, it may be nothing more. For others, this may be the only time during the week when they are connected by touch with another human being. At a fundamental level, it signals that in this community persons reach out to touch and be touched by others.

Ritual does not have just one meaning; it is *a matrix of many levels of meaning*. Thus, we can talk about a ritual being thick or dense with meaning. In addition to the sense of touching and being touched, reaching out to others to hold hands expresses the interconnectedness of this congregation. For those who know the stories and symbols of this faith community, holding hands during the benediction response symbolizes being the body of Christ, members one of another. The language of the hymn reminds the community of this meaning and interprets it to visitors.

To our understanding of ritual as a repeated pattern which points to and participates in a meaning beyond itself, we can now add three additional characteristics: something is *sensed*; some *action is taken*; some *language is used or implied*. Consider what often happens at the beginning of "An Order for Evening Prayer" (and has since at least the third century). A lamp or candle is lit and carried in; the presider says or sings "Light and peace in Jesus Christ our Lord," and the community responds, "Thanks be to God."

We sense something—there is darkness; then there is light in the darkness. An action is taken: the candle is lit and carried into the presence of the community. We hear words that clarify what is being sensed and done. There is still symbolic significance when the ritual is done in silence. But its sacramental power comes from our recognizing that it is not just for the purpose of "turning on the light" that we engage in this repeated pattern. Lighting the candle is connected with the story of Jesus, the light of the world, the light that shines in the darkness which cannot put it out, the light of the Resurrection in the darkness of the tomb. We may also connect it with Patrick's lighting of the fire on Easter eve centuries ago. Communities that have heard those words over and over will bring them to mind even when the act is done in silence.

This ritual is more than the simple, practical act of lighting a lamp when darkness falls. While it connects with the physical experience of being able to see in the light what we cannot see in the dark, it is the ritual's capacity to *evoke our participation in the stories connected with the tradition* which gives it depth, making it thick with meaning. Sociologist Emilé Durkheim teaches us that rituals are the way in which the beliefs and ideals held by the community are simultaneously *generated, experienced, and affirmed* by them. At the same time, we believe, there is a dynamic relationship between those deep insights held by the community and our individual appropriation and internalization of them.

Talking about a repeated pattern does not mean that things are done in exactly the same way every time in every place. Every evening prayer is different; every marriage ceremony is different; every baptism is different.

A memorable baptism service for us was that of Donna Sims. Donna was a student in Epworth's tutoring program and a member of our youth choir. She and three siblings had been living with an aunt who could no longer care for the children. One day they were a part of our community; the next they were gone. Members of the congregation were tenacious in working with social services until Donna and her siblings were located and we could reconnect with her. One of the families in the church sought to have Donna join their family as a foster daughter. After many months, much red tape, and lots of prayer, Donna was again a regular part of our community.

Donna told the pastor she wanted to be baptized. After preparatory conversations, the baptism was arranged. Donna's new grandfather had baptized the three other Otto children. He was honored to be asked to assist in baptizing this new granddaughter. The day arrived. Donna chose to take not one but two new names. Her new grandfather baptized her Donna Tracy (the name of her first tutor at Epworth, an Hispanic young woman who returned for this celebration) Otto (her new family's last name) Sims. Her grandfather spoke to us about the terrible wars and conflict occurring in Africa that day and the significance of what we were doing as the Otto family became, with this act, an African American/Euro-American family of God.

The service was unique; there will never be another one exactly like it. But it is not difficult to see the components of ritual in it: the repeated pattern of baptism, which points to and participates in a meaning beyond itself. We sense the water being poured into the font; there is the threefold action of placing water on Donna's head; and there is no shortage of *language* interpreting the action.

Sometimes there are so many words that they tend to obscure what we need to sense and experience. But on this day the words, the symbols, and the story we all knew (how Donna was almost lost to us but had come back to be an important part of our family of faith) were woven together. The ritual we shared graced us with the gift of the Holy Spirit.

We can learn more about ritual from studies on rituals in different cultural settings. First, the dynamic of ritual involves a *separation from the ordinary and the mundane.* Rituals are special, and engaging them involves leaving some things behind so we can attend to others.

Second, in this special ritual context, we are not bound by what we have been in the past, but we are not yet propelled into the future. This is a kind of *threshold experience.* Victor Turner talks about this being "betwixt and between" and characterizes it as having "liminality" (the Latin *limen* means "threshold"). We are no longer what we have been, and we are not yet who we will be. Here, through symbols and actions, we participate in the sacred stories that shape our identity as one of God's people.

We do this with a kind of "holy play" which puts things together in ways that are quite strange to our everyday experience. The problem is that we can become so accustomed to these actions in religious services that they seem ordinary. Whenever we take them for granted we risk missing their deep significance.

Sacramental ritual also *binds us to one another* within the community of faith. We become part of the tradition of the community. It carries us and we carry it. All this is played out on the stage of a threshold experience.

Then, as the third part in this ritual dynamic, we are *reoriented to the world* we live in day after day, but in a transformed way. We have a new sense of identity. We are a new people who are able to sing a new song. Rituals help us develop a rational and comprehensive way of giving coherence to understanding our experience. This is called our world view. At an even more basic and immediate level, ritual shapes our *ethos*—that is, our attitudes, mood, and internal motivation. When it is sacramental, ritual in the Christian context empowers us to live our "new life in Jesus Christ."

Ritual helps people focus their lives so that they know what is real and important. It helps us understand how to act in light of these priorities. It makes clear and holds us accountable for the choices we make. This is more life-changing than being conditioned or molded—it is dramatically different from indoctrination. Experience can be empowered by ritual.

Not all rituals function sacramentally for us. Sometimes they fail, becoming mere repetitive patterns with thin significance. That can be true for family rituals as well as for those celebrated by communities of faith. Empty rituals are not life-giving at all; they have a tendency to put us to sleep. They fail to be sacramental for us!

The Easter Vigil can be an embodiment of ritual with the capacity to be thick with sacramental potency. Its repeated pattern was already in place when Egeria visited Jerusalem in the early fifth century. This pattern of *Light, Word, Water,* and *Feast* clearly is not just about those things. Rather they become icons that lead us across the threshold so that we, too, can experience the paschal mystery.

As we celebrate the Easter Vigil, we gather in the darkness—the darkness of the tomb, the darkness of the world, the darkness of our lives. We enter into a time apart from the world of ordinary experience. We become aware that we arc called to leave the things that belong to that darkness behind. Here, in this sacred time and space, we kindle a new fire and light the paschal candle. We sense the light as we do at evening prayer. We rejoice in the act of the light penetrating the darkness as we hear the words "Light of Christ!" sung, and we respond by singing "Thanks be to God!"

We follow the light into the nave (it is our life pattern we are tracing), and hear the singing:

> This is the night when Jesus Christ broke the chains of death and rose triumphant from the grave, . . . when heaven is wedded to earth, and we are reconciled with God! . . . Accept this Easter candle, a flame divided but undimmed, . . . Let it mingle with the lights of heaven . . . to dispel the darkness of the night! May the Morning Star which never sets find this flame still burning.[4]

Tradition decrees that we sing this song known as the *Exsultet,* only at the Easter Vigil. This service of light is a kind of "holy play." We do not need to stand around in the darkness or follow a candle when a flip of the switch would turn on the lights. But it is more than pretending. We are participating this night in a sacramental experience that has been shared by Christians across the centuries and around the world. We, like those who have gone before, anticipate being made new as we participate with all our senses in the Easter event.

We are lifted up and carried by the stories of salvation history. This is our story, and we hear it all in the light of the resurrection faith proclaimed by the paschal candle. Then in the great sign-act of the baptismal covenant, our participation in that covenant is reaffirmed. The water placed on our foreheads in the sign of the cross incorporates us into the pattern of Christ's death and resurrection. As a community that was once "no people" but is now "God's people," we gather with the Risen Christ as our host at the great Easter banquet with the communion of saints past and present, here and everywhere. We sing with the angels; we eat with the first disciples. We are given a new way to think of ourselves. We know who we are called to be and what we are called to do. And finally we are sent forth to be a resurrection people in the midst of a world that seems bent on its own death and destruction.

A potent symbol of this connection with the everyday world is the practice of following the Easter Vigil with an Easter break-fast (in early history, the breaking of the Lenten fast). For, if we have eyes to see and ears to hear, every morning can be a celebration of the Resurrection and every break-fast a reliving of the break-fast of Easter.

What we may miss is that this understanding of ritual as an embodiment of sacramental living is not only relevant to great services of the Church such as the Easter Vigil. It is also characteristic of our family's actions when we come home from the Christmas Eve service, put the baby Jesus in the manger, hang the angel above him, and bring the shepherds to worship.

In both the Easter Vigil and this family Christmas Eve ritual, we become part of the story and it becomes a part of us. In dramatic celebrations in our communities of faith, in our homes around our kitchen tables, and on Christmas Eve, and wherever else we find ourselves, we are invited to be open to ways in which rituals kindle the fires of sacramental living in us.

Notes
1. "Thanksgiving Over the Water" from the Baptismal Covenant I, *The United Methodist Hymnal* (Nashville, Tenn.: The United Methodist Publishing House, 1989), 36.
2. The *Canticle of Simeon* from *The United Methodist Hymnal*, 225.
3. "Savior, Again to Thy Dear Name," *Pilgrim Hymnal* (Boston: The Pilgrim Press, 1958), 60.
4. An excerpt from the English translation of *Exsultet* from *The Roman Missal*.

CHAPTER FOUR

Weaving a Sacramental Fabric:

TIME & ETERNITY

Linda's mother moved this week, moved from the home she shared with her husband until his death almost two years ago. The spring Dad died, a robin built a nest in a flower box on their patio wall. Both Mother and Dad watched with interest. Fearful that either rain or the hot sun would be a problem for the mother bird and her eggs, Mother tied a big open umbrella to the trellis above the flower box so the nest would be protected. What joy they experienced, watching through the patio door as three baby robins hatched, and were fed by both father and mother robin!

Then, suddenly, unexpectedly, death came. On the day of Dad's memorial service, we watched, as the little robins left the nest, one by one, and after a few tentative and erratic attempts, flew away. Death and new life, thanksgiving and grief, memories and new possibilities were woven together.

When Carol and Paul visited us a week ago, we shared with them the simple beauty of the Sacred Heart Chapel at St. Benedict's Monastery in nearby St. Joseph, Minnesota. At the reception desk, Carol purchased the book *You Took Me In!* by Ruth Nierengarten. This book is a story with delightful drawings about a robin who built a nest on Sister Ruth's window sill, and it tells of her emotions as she watched the miracle of their birth and growth and then as she saw the baby birds (aptly named Poopsie One, Two, Three, and IV) fly away.

We returned to share in Benedictine hospitality for evening prayers and dinner the following Sunday. While we were there we bought a copy of Sister Ruth's book, told her our story, and asked her to autograph the book for Linda's mother.

The evening Mother moved from the home she and Dad had shared into her new apartment in the main building of her retirement community, she realized she hadn't thought to get the mail. Down she went to her mailbox on the first floor, and there was the book we had sent her. After reading it, she called us. "The robins in the book flew away the same day as ours," she observed. "I've found a perfect place for the book— right beside the picture of the bird under an umbrella" (a straw picture from the Philippines we had given her the Christmas after Dad died).

We usually think of time in terms of past, present, and future. But when we reflect on this story, we realize that all three are woven together to create a whole fabric. The experience cannot be adequately understood in terms of sequential time (or *chronos,* the Greek word from which we get our word *chronology*). Rather, it is an example of significant time (or *kairos,* the Greek word used in the New Testament for "fullness of time"). Certainly the memory of the birds flying away on the day of Dad's memorial service was involved, but so was the hope symbolized by the young robins heading off for new experiences. The way both of these were woven together with the testimony of an author who had watched another robin's nest, the care of family that the gift of the book signified, the context of an ending and a new beginning—all in a present moment—made the experience sacramental.

One night at The Birds' Nest, we awoke to a bright light pulsing through our bedroom window. It looked like the light of a huge searchlight coming up from the meadow beyond the next ridge. It was frightening at first. From the front deck we watched as that light separated itself into three ribbons that went all the way across the sky, descending—it seemed—into the mountains on the opposite horizon. And then those ribbons of light began to weave in and out and around one another. Fear turned to awe. Time stood still as we were entranced by the mystery of the northern lights.

Something like that happens when we experience the weave of a sacramental fabric where time and timelessness become indistinguishable. It involves remembering the past, living the present, and hoping our way into the future, but not in any linear sequence. Future expectation circles through memories even as we are acting in the present. The present is drawn into an unknown future in ways that strengthen roots to the past. The past gives us tools for meaning-sculpting in the present which becomes our past as we are catapulted into the future.

Warp . . . woof . . . loom . . . and weaver . . . ! When these come together in disciplined, creative, traditional, serendipitous, time-honored, earth-shaking ways, the results can be doorways into the sacramental.

Remembering is not something that happens in the past; it is a present activity. Nels Ferré, Dwight's theological mentor, told his classes: "There is no 'wasness' of the was; there is only an 'isness' of the was!" While true of all remembering, that is true at an even deeper level for sacramental living.

Memory is much more dynamic than we suppose. In Plato's *Phaedo*, Socrates observes that the gift of writing may be a tool for recollection, but it should not be identified with memory. Memory is dynamic, not static. It is not a calcified portrayal of the past, but the mental activity of selecting, putting together (*re*-membering), and interpreting past event in the context of a much larger picture.

A memory can become an icon, a doorway through which we perceive and by which we are drawn into the present. An icon opens us up to the realm of the Spirit, where we may be grasped by the transforming power of God's grace. Through it, God comes to us. Through it, we open ourselves to the presence of the sacred.

Is that God's work or ours? Such an either/or alternative will not do. In sacramental moments of time, we know that we are more fully invested, more completely ourselves, more involved with our whole being, than we are at any other time. But we are also aware that this *kairos*, this fullness of time, is a gift. We cannot summon it up by magic, or cause it to appear by will power. *Kairotic* time is God's weaving together of our deepest and most complete selves (mind, body, spirit, emotion, will, and all the rest) with divine grace. Like love, which is always gift but in which one also totally invests one's self, the paradox of significant and sacramental time evades precise analysis.

When the sun sets and that ball of fire drops below the horizon, many memories rush to our consciousness—

- holding Pete on that Canadian highway after he had fallen out of our van;
- discovering a heron silhouetted against the exquisite colors of the Sanibel sky;
- marveling as night falls on the waves and rocks of an Irish coast;

- and seeing the light play among the clouds at dusk at The Birds' Nest.

Sometimes, through memories like these, we become aware of God's grace in our lives and know the gift that comes to us in so many ways.

Lament can be part of remembering too. Our visit to the Nazi concentration camp at Dachau is etched into our memory. With it comes a gripping recognition of how easy it is not to see the evil around us. It is so convenient not to know. As we stood in that place where thousands died, our lament was not only for past tragedy and blindness, but for our present complicity in the evils of our own day. Lament was accompanied by commitment to both speak up and to act whenever persons are dehumanized. This moment of insight turned into resolve. This, too, is sacramental living.

This capacity of the past to interpenetrate the present is a vital part of our celebrations of the Eucharist. We hear the story and reflect again on Christ's invitation: "Do this in remembrance of me." What does it mean to "remember Jesus?" While we recall the story of the Last Supper, the prayer of Thanksgiving sets that recollection within the context of Christ's life, death, and resurrection. Our center of attention is not a dead Jesus who lived nearly two thousand years ago, but the risen Christ, present with us and among us here and now. The past invades the present with potential for nourishing us and empowering our discipleship. By remembering, we enter the story ourselves. The past event becomes present power. Indeed, it is not so much a past event as a present experience of the immediacy of Christ's life, death, and resurrection. All of this is woven together with our sense of Christ's presence, here and now, and our participation in this reality as a part of the body of Christ in this time and place.

Ruth Duck, our friend and colleague at the seminary, wrote a hymn, *Give Thanks to the Source*, that captures this understanding:

Give thanks to the Source who brings forth earth's goodness:
the bread on our table, the fruit of the vine.
Give thanks to the Love who welcomes the wand'ring,
invents new beginnings, and calls us to dine.

Remember the Word, incarnate among us,
whose table is open to all who draw near.
Recall Jesus Christ in living and dying,
in rising to new life, set free from our fear.

We pray for the gift of life-giving Spirit
that we may know Jesus in sharing this meal.
So may we depart refreshed for the journey,
to live by the Gospel, to love and to heal.[2]

It is possible to get stuck in the past, either because we idealize it and think we want to keep living it over and over again, or because we cannot seem to let go of its pain. The past is usually not as wonderful as memory paints it. The New Testament church is not a model of how everything ought to be (just read 1 Corinthians!). Dwight's father used to say that the reason people think youth are going to the dogs is because they don't remember their own dog days!

The desire to "just go back to the good old days" is the result of selective memory. Even if it were as good as we think it was (and it wasn't!), transporting the past into the present without regard for current context won't work. Times have changed and are changing. Those who try to enter the twenty-first century by returning to what life was like in the 1950s have chosen an impossible path.

Nor is it desirable to let the pain of the past prevent us from living in the present. This is easy to write and most would agree with it. We know all too well there are times when it is not easy to live! Wounds from the past cannot just be buried. They keep recycling through our lives, often in pain-filled and destructive ways, blind-siding us at unexpected times. Naming old wounds and finding therapists and spiritual directors to help us know how to deal with them has been an important part of our journey toward sacramental living.

Over and over, we discover we need to pray: "Grant us the serenity to accept the things we cannot change, the courage to change the things we can, and the wisdom to know the difference." For us, living out that prayer is hard work. If we are to engage life in sacramental ways, it is work we must learn to do.

We have a framed quotation on our bathroom wall that reads: "Never let yesterday use up today." It reminds us that we can let the joys and opportunities of the present be obscured by holding too tightly to the hurts we have experienced in the past. The challenge of sacramental living is to receive the legacy of the past, good and bad, to learn from it, and be motivated by it, without being enslaved. After all, as Shakespeare declared in *The Tempest*, "What's past is prologue."

Believing "the past is what it is, and there's no doing anything about it" enslaves us. It is true that we can't go back and will that the events themselves happen in a different way. But when we remember that it is the "isness of the was" which is making its impact in the present, we discover that we are actively involved in a dynamic sculpting of meaning in the here and now. The interpretation and appropriation of the past is not fixed in concrete. We can learn to see in new ways, to color outside the lines.

As a seven-year-old, Dwight's vivid memory of his grand-father lying dead on the blood-soaked stubble in that farm field was the source of troubled dreams. On the day of the funeral, the roads near the country church were filled with cars. The church was over-flowing. After the committal service, folks began to share their reasons for coming: "We would have lost the farm if it hadn't been for Chris." "Our crops would have been lost when Pop was laid up if Chris hadn't helped us." "We'd never have made it through the depression without Chris."

Among those present were two Catholic priests (this was in 1944, long before Vatican II, when Catholics and Protestants had little to do with each other). "All week long people have been talking about the tragic death of Chris Vogel and how much he'd meant to them, so we said to each other: 'If he really touched our people's lives like that, we ought to go to his funeral.'" Gradually this remembered story was linked with the dreadful memory. Years later, the relationship of images from the Eucharist (bread, broken body, shed blood) and that boy-hood experience combined to provide a new way of inter-preting and appropriating that past event. His grandpa's bro-ken body became an icon for internalizing the meaning of Christ's body broken for all.

Henri Nouwen encourages us to believe and act on the reality that each moment of our life is "pregnant with new life." That is an awesome idea. If each moment is pregnant with new life, our task in the present becomes one of learn-ing how to be midwives! The miracle of new birth is still a gift, but we can learn how to open ourselves to receive this gift and how to assist rather than thwart the birthing process in others.

Maria Harris uses the midwife metaphor for understanding our identity as teachers. To be a midwife teacher (or a midwife friend or preacher or parent or partner) is to recognize that what is being birthed in another is theirs—not ours. Our task is to assist them in giving birth to their new moment; it is to encourage and support and challenge and to "be there" no matter what! We are challenged to accept the gift other midwives offer us as we give birth to new life and new days.

Helen Keller's teacher, Annie Sullivan, took her by the hand into the sunshine, placed Helen's hand under the flowing water from the spout of the pump, and then began spelling W-A-T-E-R in the palm of her other hand. She was the midwife. But it was Helen, blind and deaf from nineteen months of age, who experienced the reality of her own new life as she recalls in *The Story of My Life*: "That living word, awakened my soul, gave it light, hope, joy, set it free!"

How often we move through the present as if we were being propelled through each day as one who is strapped into the tilt-a-whirl at the amusement park. Life is full of jerks and starts; it is exciting and scary. It seems totally out of our control, like the tilt-a-whirl, on tracks that others have laid. This debilitating feeling is reflected in the not uncommon remark, "Things are a mess; but there's nothing I can do about it!"

This is nothing new, however, as one discovers by reading books like Edward Rutherfurd's historical novel, *Sarum*, which follows the saga of five families who lived near what is now Salisbury, England from prehistory into the present. The scenery changes, problems take on different shapes, but facing questions of meaning, confronting conflicting loyalties, dealing with issues of power, and learning to live in community are universal human tasks. We can't do everything, but we can do something!

When we were traveling in India with our friend Father David Fleming, he was invited to celebrate a Eucharist with some novices of the Sisters of Charity who had just arrived from Bombay. After mass, we had the unforgettable experience of talking with Mother Teresa. We remember savoring that time: the sunlight on the balcony, her wise and wrinkled face with piercing eyes, the sisters in the courtyard below doing laundry, and her parting words, "Please pray for us that we will be faithful, and not interfere with God's work."

In the immediacy of that moment, we were given a gift—and that gift involved what we should and could do (be "faithful"), and what we shouldn't do ("interfere with God's work"). She truly believed that she and her sisters—whose devotion to God and care of the rejected and dying ones in our world is legendary—needed to be aware of this possibility and to guard against getting in the way of God's work. Those who criticize Mother Teresa for not attacking the systemic problems that cause persons to be sick and hungry and dying on the streets of Calcutta and Chicago may be called to do that very thing. But Mother's calling was to share compassion and love and to feed and hold the dying. Each of us must discern and answer our own unique call.

Mother Teresa's request presupposes that God is active and that we only muck up the situation when we forget that our understanding is partial. We must avoid the temptation to play God!

Zacchaeus could only be faithful by returning to his tax collecting and doing it honestly; Matthew was called to leave his tax collecting behind to follow Jesus. The Geresene demoniac wanted to follow Jesus, but Jesus told him to return home and witness there to what God had done; the rich young ruler's call was to leave home and follow Jesus. Whenever we feel sure that we are right, that our beliefs are truly God's beliefs, that our way is the way for someone else to be faithful, we depart from the paths of sacramental living.

We are often kept from sacramental living by our busyness,

our absorbing concern with many things. We spend a great deal of time and energy on what seems, at the moment, so very pressing! As Harold Beck used to say: "We are so busy with the urgent that we have no time for the important." If we would not interfere with God's work, we must take time to follow the injunction that used to be on all railway crossings: "Stop! Look! Listen!" If we are too busy talking, planning, and doing, we will be unable to attend to our being.

Being is more fundamental than doing. Taylor and June McConnell have helped us appropriate this deep insight which they learned from the pueblo peoples. The January we were in the Santa Fe area learning that lesson, Dwight was trying to decide what to do. His responsibilities at the seminary had grown, and he still held a position as minister of music at Northbrook United Methodist Church. He had accepted the invitation to join the staff there when he was still trying to put together a full time job. It was fulfilling and rewarding work. There was a talented and committed choir, a warm and caring congregation, and the opportunity to preach and celebrate the sacraments.

But one day, while walking to the central plaza in Santa Fe, something clicked. He remembers: "I discovered I was asking the wrong question. As long as I focused on what I should do the answer was unclear. But as soon as I changed it to how I am to be, the solution became crystal clear. I was fragmented and unfocused. I was trying to live two lives and my primary calling was to the seminary community. Therefore, I needed to resign a much loved position so that I could be who I am called to be."

Dwight still misses the Northbrook choir, just as he misses the congregation he served as pastor in Dubuque. But in order to "not interfere with God's work," one must get out of the way of one's soul! In the sacramental life, *being* has priority over *doing*. We cannot attend to the present if life is brim full of activity. Zen Buddhist masters teach us that unless we empty our cup, enlightenment cannot come. We must attend to the here and now, rather than being distracted by the there and then.

John Stanley Eng was committed to honoring the lifelines of the wood he sculpted. "A sculptor has to know when to stop," he used to say. Doing may be part of our responsibility, but we have to know when to stop, when trying to do more will accomplish less, when we need to "let our souls catch up with our bodies."

Busy people are often advised: "Take time to smell the flowers!" What that means varies from person to person. What nourishes one is only another thing to do for someone else. A useful spiritual discipline may be to examine how we define "wasting time." Sometimes it is in the quiet times—when we lay in our hammock and watch the clouds, or sit in our living room and watch the darkness of the night begin to replace the last of the sun's rays, or relax in the bathtub full of bubbles—that we are using our time most wisely! Times that seem to be "good for nothing" may be good times in and of themselves.

Dwight tells the members of the seminary choir he directs, "If the music we sing nourishes you and feeds you spiritually, then the busier you are with schoolwork, the more you will discover you need singing in the choir to provide needed strength for the journey! If, on the other hand, singing in the choir doesn't feed your soul, you will probably discover you don't have time and it will be just one more thing you ought not take on!"

Even after our children left home and there were just the two of us, mornings often felt like the race had begun and we were already behind! By the time we got up, showered, dressed, had breakfast, dealt with the dirty dishes, and got our "stuff" together, we found ourselves rushing breathlessly out the door. The pattern for the rest of the day tended to feel like we were falling further and further behind. Linda treasured the time on our days off when we would take our coffee into the bay window of our living room, lean back in recliners, and take time to be. We decided that we would try to carve out five minutes each morning before we left for the seminary to do just that. Most mornings we manage to do it. While at Collegeville, we took time to go out on the patio, mug in hand, to greet the morning. After the snow came, we were content to greet it from inside looking out! Taking even a few minutes *to be* makes all the difference in the world in how we face the day.

Dwight has discovered that when he listens to the news up until the time we leave, the troubles and discontent of the world seem to be replicated in his soul. After hearing the news, he needs to be nourished with music in order to have strength for the journey of the day. Linda, on the other hand, feels connected to the world by listening to the news; without it, she feels less a citizen of the global village.

We have created a routine that seems to address both our needs. We wake up to National Public Radio. When Dwight goes into the kitchen to get breakfast, he turns on the classical music station. Meanwhile, in the bedroom and bathroom, Linda continues to hear the news. Sharing morning prayers together at the breakfast table after we have eaten sets the framework for the day ahead.

The only complication arises when someone is in our guest room and gets news from one direction and music from another! We try to be sensitive, but more often than not, our routine carries us through. We never know what we've done to the souls of our guests in their preparation for the day!

Individuals and families need to recognize that we are fed in different ways. We must try to find ways we can honor both our own ways of nourishing our soul and the ways others need for nourishing theirs, so none of us will "interfere with God's work." Finding time and space to nurture our spiritual connections, and respecting others whose connections are nourished in ways different from our own, are both important aspects of living sacramentally.

Another piece of folk wisdom that is a key to sacramental living in the present says, "Bloom where you are planted!" The words may have become trite but the concept is profound. It has to do with the "being faithful" part of Mother Teresa's prayer request. For as long as one's heart is somewhere other than in the here and now, its potential for sacramental life cannot be realized. We miss the pregnancy of the moment and the new life it brings.

That does not mean that we are called to invest ourselves without reservation, come what may. For twenty years, we lived in Le Mars, Iowa, and taught at Westmar College. They were good years. We were able to make a difference in many students' lives and they made a difference in ours. We had stimulating and supportive colleagues. But when the situation changed and a different administrative approach caused us to have increasing reservations, we knew our ministry needed to be lived out in a different place.

When we are no longer able to bloom where we are planted, we must either check out possibilities for transplanting or see if the application of fertilizer can nurture new life where we are. Like all good advice, "bloom where you are planted" can become an excuse for not dealing with changing realities in the present and for not taking responsibility for the future. What is right today may not be right for us tomorrow. Our *being* and our *doing* must always be offered to the Spirit and that means we must be open to change.

Whenever we are in London, we plan to attend evensong

at Saint Paul's Cathedral. The music is an experience of the transcendent. But if you were to ask Dwight if he sees even-song there as a good model for others to follow, he would respond, "No." A crucial component for him, namely the active participation of the worshipers, is lacking. However, it would do no good to fuss and fume inwardly about that fact and thereby miss the gift the marvelous music that fills that wonderful cathedral is making. Learning to accept as gift what others offer, without always focusing on how our way of doing it would be better, allows us to receive sacramentally the gifts and ministry of others.

We remember hearing this story during our seminary days. When Dietrich Bonhoeffer was teaching at the underground seminary at Finkenwald, he was asked how he dealt with all the services led by students and colleagues with widely varying styles and abilities. "There is really only one important question to ask about each service," he replied. "What is God saying to me in this service?"

Following that advice can free us to find nourishment in a wide variety of services. It keeps us from majoring in negativity, and it allows us to open ourselves to the icons through which God is speaking. When we are in a given service, that is where we are planted. God is never without some witness. If we can get by the things that are distracting us, we may discover, even in the midst of things and ways of acting we don't approve, that the fullness of God's time can grasp us in that moment.

Living our baptism! That's what sacramental living is all about. For baptism celebrates God's grace. God reaches out to us, claims and supports us, and cares for us. But baptism is also about being marked with the sign of the cross, about living faithfully. It is about being disciples of Jesus Christ—learners, disciplined ones seeking to "grow in the grace and knowledge" of the One whose name we bear.

What I am called to be and to do in each present moment is crucial. The important question is not "When were you baptized?' Rather, we are called to respond to "Are you living your baptism?"

As we have seen, baptism connects us with the story. Through baptism, we are incorporated into the death and resurrection of Jesus Christ. There is much that "dying with Christ and being raised with Christ" compels us to be and do in our present living. At the same time, it also pulls us into a future that is not yet. "Your kingdom come," we pray. But when we look around—at our world, at our church, and at ourselves—we are keenly aware of the great distance between what we see and the rule and reign of God to which we are called.

The vision of God's kin-dom (of what it means to be God's family, of what God wants all humankind to be and do) invades the present and pulls us toward the future we believe God intends. Our baptism commissions us to claim our role as co-creators with God—witnessing to God's justice-love and graceful-compassion in our hurtful and hurting world.

Just as the past can be in the present moment, so the future can transform the present. Without that vision of hope, without that sense of the future actually manifesting itself in the present, our attempts at faithful living become much more difficult.

One of Linda's advisees, Lois Bucher, helps us see how the story of one's baptism can weave future, present, and past together in powerful ways. It demonstrates how living the story of our baptism may lead us into places we never intended to go.

Lois says it seems as though she really remembers that Sunday morning when she was baptized as an infant, because her godmother and her family have told and re-told the story of that day. "I don't know what I wore and I don't even have any pictures of the special event," she says. "I was not sprinkled or dunked. I was kissed into the Christian faith!" Her pastor, Harold Wilke, "was born without arms; but he was one of the least handicapped people I have ever known. Pastor Wilke dipped his lips into the font and then he kissed my forehead," she says. From her earliest memory, Lois has always known that she is loved by God and by the church. She continues to know that she belongs!

Lois became a teacher of young children. She worked as an active volunteer teacher and Christian educator in her congregation. But gradually she came to understand that she needed to attend seminary to be better prepared to teach the faith. That process began to love her into accepting her call to become a pastor who teaches and who loves folks in her congregation into the faith. So after twenty years of public school teaching, she was ordained as a minister in the United Church of Christ and is walking into a future of ministering through her church in God's name.

A wonderful fabric of time and eternity was woven in Chicago following the death of Joseph Cardinal Bernardin. Cardinal Bernardin chose to share his dying as he had shared his life with the people of his city and the world. In humility and honesty, he shared his feelings and his journey toward death so that others might be blessed on their own journeys. It was amazing to be in Chicago in the week following his death as people of all faiths—and those who claimed no faith community at all—talked, cried, and mourned together.

Our colleague at St. John's, Kathleen Hughes, also lives in Chicago but our lives had not touched until we three became scholars in residence at the Ecumenical Institute. On the day of the first anniversary of Joseph Cardinal Bernardin's death, Kathleen shared an article she had felt compelled to write as she experienced her own grief a year ago. She wrote,

> Standing in that line and later sitting in the Cathedral and watching all of humanity stream by was an experience I will not soon forget. Every possible person from every walk of life and in every conceivable circumstance was drawn to the Cathedral. A homeless man dragging all his possessions was followed by a woman in a mink coat; babies in arms and elderly using walkers came up the aisle; young children were lifted to see his face; every nationality, ethnic group, color, and religion were represented among the mourners. Men and women with briefcases followed those with back packs; city workers came and their hard hats were doffed in his direction. Those who most moved my heart were the sick, particularly the children who were obviously being ravaged by cancer and chemo-therapy. The line of mourners took two days to move by his bier and the city estimates that at least 100,000 people braved sub-freezing temperatures and a wait of sometimes two hours just to walk by the one that everyone now called "our brother Joseph."[1]

On the day of the funeral, Kathleen attended morning prayer at the Cathedral. When the Secret Service evacuated the church to prepare for Vice President Al Gore's arrival, she made her way to a nearby coffee shop to wait. There she found a man "holding forth about 'Father Bernadin'—how he had written courageously about war and peace and had taken a stand against nuclear armament. The man recalled shaking the Cardinal's hand and thanking him and he spoke to any who would listen about the joy of that encounter. Then he declared: 'Maybe now when people think of Chicago, they will think of Al Capone AND Father Bernardin.'"

Weaving a sacramental fabric of life becomes an invitation to embrace *kairotic* moments as we seek to dance—as if around a May pole—weaving past and future into the present moment. We marvel at the differing colors and hues that others bring and that the sunlight and the moonlight shed on our own colors and hues. This dance requires openness and a graciousness that receives what others offer even as we offer our own gifts.

Sacramental living impels us to acknowledge that the fabric we share in weaving is one that embraces great joys and deep pains; it embraces things we love and things not to our liking. But in the end, many colors and textures blend, by God's grace, to make the whole. This fabric which weaves together time and eternity is not an escape from human relationships. It draws us into multiple connections with the global village—relating us with all God's children and, indeed, with the whole creation. It compels us to "pray that we will be faithful and not interfere with God's work."

Notes
1. Kathleen Hughes, RSCJ, "Joseph Cardinal Bernardin: Reflection on his life and his death."

CHAPTER FIVE

Breaking Bread with Com-pan-ions:

COMMUNITY

O ver thirty years ago Linda's parents sent us the telephone number of a son of Ambrose and Mildred Fleming. Ambrose had been a friend of Linda's father since childhood. The two families remained friends across the years though they never discussed religion. The Flemings were Roman Catholic, and Linda's family was protestant in a time when such differences were thought to be best left alone.

We were in graduate school and David was doing doctoral studies at another institution in the Chicago area. They suggested we try to get together. David was a brother of the Society of Mary. Our contacts with Roman Catholics had been few in number and superficial in nature. We decided to invite him for lunch. He accepted.

We can still see him in his black suit climbing the stairs to our tiny third-floor apartment. We later learned he was as apprehensive as we were! We sat down to lunch, "broke bread together," and began to talk. At 5:30 we were still at the table, so we exchanged lunch dishes for supper ones, and kept talking—about matters of faith and church structure, the sacraments and our spiritual journeys. We were hungry for the honesty, integrity, and openness we found in each other.

We have since broken bread together in LeMars, Iowa, and Topeka, Kansas, in San Antonio and St. Louis, in Rome and Bangalore, in Geneva and Taizé, and in countless other places. Last summer, we broke bread on the front deck of The Birds' Nest and prayed for his work as the newly elected head of his order. We are com-pan-ions and our faith journey is greatly enriched.

When we visited our eldest son Mark and his family in Spain, we delighted in the usual breakfast menu wherever we went: a small loaf of pan and a cup of coffee con leche. *Pan* means "bread," *com* means "with;" thus, companions are those with whom we share bread.

We experience companionship at different levels and in many ways. Companionship characterizes the intimate personal partnership arising from the covenant we made before God and with one another through marriage. It can characterize any covenant relationship made between persons.

At St. John's Abbey and St. Benedict's Monastery, we observe the companionship that results when persons enter a religious community with whom they choose to cast their lot and share their life. Abbot Timothy was reflecting on the importance of koinonia (community) for Benedictine spirituality. "Our vow of stability is not only to a place," he observed. "It is a vow of stability of relationship to each other in community. We must be dependable for one another.

"Diversity, if it is not recognized as valuable, will destroy community. Just as the penance of marriage is living in family relationships, so the penance of a monastic community is living in community!

"Community needs complementarity rather than uniformity. The complementarity resulting from our diversity has sign value. It expresses to the world the possibility of peace and unity despite difference. For me, the community is a sign of reconciliation in the world, for we have to actualize that reconciliation in the community."

Companionship also characterizes the deep and abiding friendships in our lives and marks small groups with whom we share in significant ways. Breaking bread with others is central to our life in the Church. The ripples of companionship move out even farther when we recognize that we are bound to those we do not know, because we break bread with One who breaks bread with them. All who accept Jesus Christ's invitation to come to the Table are bound together with us as members of the Body of Christ.

There is potential for the sacramental in all of these if we have eyes to see and ears to hear and hearts to love. Bernard Cooke adds to Christ and the Church a third basic sacrament— human friendship. Through companioning we receive grace. We receive this gift with gratitude and are transformed by it. There is always something of mystery in it. We cannot fully understand it or explain it. companioning can be an icon through which we come to know and experience God's presence in our lives.

Nowhere is the gift of grace more apparent to the two of us than in the intimate personal partnership we share. In the first glow of discovering that special person who is such a delight to us, we are amazed to discover that not only are we noticed, we are valued and treasured. We seek ways to spend time together, to share our stories and our lives, to treasure what the other finds significant. We become important to each other, a special person with special value that brings delight and joy.

The wonder is that having broken bread with each other as life partners for forty years, and being known by our partner through and through (often better than we know ourselves), the gift of love still comes. It continues to become richer and deeper than we ever thought possible.

While the first blush of love sees only the good in the beloved ("love is blind," they say!), mature love is very much aware of faults, failures, and frustrations. We love in spite of that which mars the goodness in each other. Nor is the ongoing nature of this gift the result of any guarantee. Many of the couples with whom we have been friends across the years are divorced. This is not to imply that we are better persons or that we have worked harder at our marriage than they have (although it has taken work, to be sure). It is a mystery, and one for which we are deeply grateful, that the gift of our love for each other continues to bless us. It enables our companionship to survive the difficult times we go through.

Our relationship is a sacrament to us of the love of God. That love always surprises us. We did not earn it or deserve it. God's love just comes as a gift. Nor is God's love blind, but love that is aware of our failures—failures that sometimes cause heart-rending pain. God's love impels us to embody this way of being together.

A quote attributed to George Eliot hangs on our wall: "Oh, the comfort, the inexpressible comfort, of feeling safe with a person, having neither to weigh thoughts nor measure words, but pouring them all right out just as they are, chaff and grain together, certain that a faithful hand will take and sift them, keeping what is worth the keeping, and with the breath of kindness blow the rest away." We have since learned that Dinah Maria Mulock Craik wrote these words in *A Life for a Life*. No matter who wrote the words, we value the sacramental meaning of this statement.

We are not all that we could be; we are not all that we should be. Even so, God reaches out to us and assures us we are special; even the hairs on our head are worth God's attention!

There is more to it than "feeling good" about each other and liking to spend time together. When our delight in each other is fractured, and one of us causes the other pain, we discover that caring and companionship not only continue, but they are strengthened as we listen and speak the truth to one another. That is the way God loves us, reaching beyond our sin to our pain. We are accepted as we are, it is true, but we are not left there. Because we are loved and valued, we open ourselves to the power of the Holy Spirit who transforms us and empowers us to grow toward wholeness—both individually and as a couple.

In the most intimate expressions of love, the sacrament of giving ourselves to each other leads us to rejoice in the other's joy more than in seeking our own pleasure. Beyond that (not always, but frequently) there emerges a deep sense of sharing oneness, not only with each other but also with God. These sacramental moments are gifts beyond words.

The bread we break, the lives we share, become for us a participation in God's love and care. Even when life reflects this reality imperfectly, we find in intimate personal partnership a doorway to the sacred. Our love, freely given and received, nourishes us and invites us into sacramental living in our everyday activities.

Deep and abiding friendships come both as gift and as the result of on-going investment on both sides. We have marveled at friendships that developed over twenty years in LeMars and that continue and even deepen as we nourish them across the miles.

One evening after vespers (a service Dwight led weekly at Westmar College), we decided to drop in on a new faculty member and his wife. We all came from Kansas and knew folks in common. Our shared cultural background signaled that it would probably be all right to drop in unannounced. Joan made a pot of tea (!); we began to talk. Sitting around their kitchen table, a deep friendship was born.

When we sit down to share a cup of tea with Bob and Joan now, the conversation takes off as though we had never been apart. We talk about our children, what retirement might mean for each of us, our extended families, and our faith. We laugh; we cry. We pray and share the worry over impending surgery and ongoing health concerns. No topic is off-limits as we share what matters most to each of us.

We flew to Minnesota two years ago to participate in the marriage of their younger daughter. When Marcia introduced us to her fiancé, she said: "They've been part of my family longer than I have!" And it is true!

When Dwight was a student in an undergraduate philosophy seminar, he went for help on a difficult chapter to Ellen Oliver, the mathematics professor. When we returned to teach at his alma mater, a friendship began to grow with Ellen and her husband Eldon. They became for us a blend of surrogate family, wise mentor, academic colleague, and warm friends. "Aunt Ellen" and "Uncle Eldon" loved our children and befriended Linda's widowed mother when she came to Le Mars to live.

Ellen has the gift of discernment and forthright communication. One day she said to Linda: "I don't know what you're taking, but I don't like what it's doing to you." Linda realized she didn't like it either, went home and flushed the valium the doctor had given her down the toilet (in the late sixties, that seemed to be the prescription of choice when women went to their doctors!).

Dwight was reeling from disappointment, frustration and embarrassment when, at his oral defense, his doctoral dissertation was returned for revision. For six months, Ellen and Eldon (along with many of our other faculty colleagues) supported and strengthened us. Then one day, Ellen met Dwight on the sidewalk and asked if he had begun work on the revisions yet. He admitted he hadn't. She looked him in the eye, and with kindly firmness said: "You've had long enough to recover. It's time for you to get back to work." It was; he did; and we were grateful for the wisdom which deep friendship could share without judgment. Ellen knows how to speak the truth frankly and in love. Her truth-telling is often sacramental—"a word from God."

Twenty years in Le Mars, Iowa, cemented friendships that extend beyond the grave. But we continue to marvel that three years as ministers at St. Luke's United Methodist Church in Dubuque gifted us with friendships equally deep and lasting.

The telephone helps us stay in touch; we write letters sometimes and e-mail is a great bridge-builder. Friendships thrive when folks are intentional and nurture them. But the bottom line seems to be that our lives are connected in ways that invite deep sharing. We can talk about the deep hurts and the great joys that our children bring. We can brag about our (adult) children and our grandchildren—knowing that our friends rejoice with us. Paul and Carol are such friends. We know that no matter where either of us lives, we make the effort and take the time to be together because our friendship—the companioning we share—is a sacred gift.

Jim and Mary have shared their lives with us, and we, too, find ways to nurture and sustain that deep friendship. It was already firmly in place when their teen-aged daughter, Jennifer, was killed in a tragic accident. The story of how they and their church community dealt with that death was one Linda believed should be shared. As she worked with the them, writing *Rituals for Resurrection*, the friendship deepened. We know how to laugh together (that happens often), but we can also cry together. The words of the hymn have a new depth of meaning: "Blest be the tie that binds our hearts in Christian love."

Sometimes a friendship is born almost instantly, full-blown. Taylor and June McConnell had been faculty at Garrett-Evangelical before we came. We saw them at conferences and enjoyed visiting with them. They invited us to stay with them in Santa Fe. We love that area and decided to believe that they really meant what they said. We wrote a tentative letter saying we were coming over spring break and would enjoy spending time with them if that were convenient. We would rent a car and hope not to inconvenience them.

Their gracious reply indicated that they would meet our train. We began by having lunch together—breaking bread—and the conversation and sharing never stopped. Our rental car sat in their driveway most days except when we drove them on a joint trip to Taos one day. The connection the four of us shared was a gift that surprised us all. That friendship continues to nourish us in profound ways for these friends are wise and wonderful! We continue to nurture this friendship in Chicago and in Santa Fe.

There are countless others who have graced our lives with friendship. Friends sometimes become family for us. Our friend Joy, who lives in the Black Hills, spent an Easter with us in Dubuque and flew to Chicago to attend Kris and Bill's wedding. We have walked with each other through some painful and difficult times. Even though we rarely write and only occasionally talk on the phone, we know that what we have is real and will last forever. We know we can count on one another.

The depth of the sharing is what marks true friendship and separates it from other relationships. When we walk through the valley of the shadow of death with others, a strong bond is forged. Willingly investing time and energy in relationships nourishes them and keeps them alive. Knowing that we will speak the truth to one another builds trust. Raising hard questions and knowing that we can still count on the steadfastness of the relationship brings a sense of safety and comfort.

Friendships often embody moments which are sacramental. We become aware that God is present in our relationship and graces us through it. Together with these friends we have faced tragic deaths, the imprisonment of a loved one, the facing together of life-threatening illnesses, deep concern over the welfare of our children, anguish over what was happening in our faith communities, and so much more. We have shared the marriages of our children and the pain of divorce. We have celebrated the gift of birth and the anguish of death that came much too soon.

When there are no words, there can be hugs. There can be a caring glance and a time just to be—in silence—together. When God created friendship, the world became a more hospitable place and the possibility of sacramental living was born.

Deep friendship is inherently sacramental. Companioning is valuable in and of itself, but that value is not exhausted by what can be outwardly observed. Breaking bread together is not valued merely because we receive physical nourishment. As we journey through life, breaking bread together serves as a metaphor for all the sharing we do: stories, pain, joy, sorrow, concerns, anticipation, actions, beliefs, differences, intentions, regrets. As we break bread together, we share our lives.

In deep and sacramental friendship, these expressions of companioning both point to and participate in dynamic personal relationships. We go beyond our ordinary ways of interacting with others. We perceive in a different way, experiencing more than what is immediately apparent. We receive from beyond ourselves—we each receive more than either of us gives. In companioning we experience more than the sum of the personal investment we make.

We are transformed in ways that give new meaning to each of our lives and to the relationship we share.

In our companioning we experience God's Spirit gracing our friendship. God's grace is not a thing, but the personal sharing of love. When we experience others opening themselves to us and sharing out of the depths of their being, even as we are able to open ourselves to them, we begin to understand and receive God's grace in new and life-giving ways.

A story from the Gospels illuminates this. Jesus sat at a table with the disciples in Emmaus (Luke 24:13-35). As they broke bread together, the disciples' eyes were opened, and they recognized Christ was with them. Once they were aware of that presence, they remembered how their hearts were "burning within." When we become aware of the sacramental nature of deep friendships, we may recognize the presence of Christ who has been present all along, walking with us on the road as we travel together and receive grace from each other.

God's grace is offered to us in small groups that incorporate persons who may never become best friends. One such group for us was the Inquirers Sunday School class at Calvary Church in Le Mars, Iowa. When we moved to LeMars to teach at Westmar College in 1965, this was the young adult class. We met in a third floor classroom under the sloping roof of the church.

There were about thirty members of this class—men and women, married and single. Our identity was defined by the assertion that "there is no subject that is out of bounds and no question that cannot be asked. The only thing one must have to join this class is an open mind!"

We discussed many topics over the twenty years we belonged to this group. We watched one member die of brain cancer and tried to help her husband and sons cope with her long illness and death. Members of our group gave birth, adopted children, experienced the loss of a child, divorced, lost jobs, worried over the struggles of teenage children, ran for political office, experienced the pain of moving away, and much, much more.

The Inquirers knew how to have a party. We had progressive dinners and Watch Night parties on New Year's Eve. During a hobo party, when we were drinking cider out of cans down by the train tracks, someone called the police—they thought some college students were partying. The dean of students was quick to set the record straight, though the police were surprised at his hobo attire! We worked on service projects together, broke bread together, had fun together, and discussed endlessly. But the bottom line was we knew and cared about each other and would be there for each other, whatever needs emerged.

We could tell you some of the topics we studied; we could describe in detail a dozen memorable parties we had. But when we think about the Inquirers Sunday School class, we experience a warm feeling welling up in our hearts, and we know without a shadow of a doubt that these members of Christ's body knew us well—the good and bad—and would be there for us through thick and thin. There were funny times and deeply painful times. But through it all, God's presence and unmerited gift of acceptance was embodied by those of us who grew too old to climb those stairs. When we moved away there were three newer classes known successively as "the young adults" in that church.

Our experiences of small groups that embody sacramental living for us and with us are many. There is the local chapter of the Order of Saint Luke for Dwight, and his lectionary study group in Dubuque. A group of Christian education professors in Chicago and the women faculty at Garrett-Evangelical are significant for Linda.

We both have shared in the United Methodist Association of

Scholars in Christian Education biennial consultations—most often at Estes Park in the Rocky Mountains—since 1974. Families were included and friendships forged, not only among the adults, but among our children as well. Sacramental moments are shared with these colleagues and friends as we wrestle with hard issues, experience the awe of traveling up Fall River Road toward the sky, worship, and break bread together.

During the past ten years we have shared in a covenant group with Christian colleagues in Chicago. The group meets monthly for dinner in one of our homes. We share what is happening in our lives, talk about what concerns us, and pray for one another, our work, the church, and our world. Two couples moved away. When one couple divorced, one of them chose to leave the group. We have incorporated two new couples into the group. We gather to go to a concert at Ravinia each summer and to watch fireworks on the shore of Lake Michigan on the Fourth of July. Participation in the group is a high priority for all of us. Although many members of the group have schedules that make setting our group meetings a challenge, none of us wants to miss the deep sharing and the knowledge that we can talk about our fears and hopes in a safe and hospitable place.

In such groups, our understanding of the sacramental is enlarged. We often become aware that the struggles we share are not unlike those shared by others who may not have a supporting community to share their pains, joys, and concerns. The small group is a doorway into life beyond the sensory and the rational. Lives are enriched when persons risk sharing their journey with com-pan-ions.

Some persons walk their journey hand in hand with us; others are part of the pilgrimage in significant but less intimate ways. We know we are all on the journey together. We break bread in countless ways. We are companions, and that reality nourishes us for our journey. Whenever we experience the presence of God in our midst, see and hear God's call to journey in faith toward God's kin-dom, we know that we are blessed to be walking the path of sacramental living.

Breaking bread with others is central to our life in the Church. Children, as well as youth and adults, often sing the Avery and Marsh song: "I am the church! You are the church! We are the church together!" At a young age, they are beginning to realize that the church is more than a building; it is made up of many different people and they are included.

Children often have eyes to see and ears to hear while the adults around them may act as though they are blind and deaf. When our son was five he responded to our pastor's invitation to the Lord's table—given to all who love Jesus and want to accept his invitation to come—with a penetrating question. "I love Jesus, Mommy," he whispered. "Why can't I go?"

It was a fair question but our Evangelical United Brethren Church practiced the custom of having children wait until after catechism to participate in holy communion. We talked with Peter after church and suggested that he talk with Pastor Tom about what communion means. So one day after kindergarten, Peter walked the three blocks to the church and met with our pastor. When he came home, he said, "Pastor Tom says I can have communion now." "That's good," we responded, and Peter went out to play.

The next time we saw the pastor he asked us what we knew about octopus. Puzzled, we wondered why he asked! Pastor Tom said, "When I asked Peter what he thought happened at communion, he told me that he thought God was like a big octopus with lots of arms. God stands in the center aisle and wraps everyone in arms of love at the same time." To this day, none of us has a clue about where that metaphor came from, but as our pastor said, "Would that all our adults understood that!"

One of Linda's favorite gospel stories is of Jesus feeding the five thousand. It shows us clearly that whatever questions we bring, Jesus usually re-frames them. The disciples were exhausted, and instead of promised quiet time and rest, Jesus had compassion for the crowd that followed them and spent the afternoon healing and teaching.

Finally as evening approached, the disciples urged Jesus to send the crowd away. When Jesus tells them that they should give the crowd something to eat, they ask in astonishment, "Are we to go and buy two hundred denarii (one denarii was a farm laborer's daily wage) worth of bread and give it to them to eat?" Jesus re-frames the question: "How many loaves have you? Go and see." That huge crowd is soon sitting on the grass in small groups (there are those important small groups again!). Jesus *takes* the bread, looks up to heaven, *blesses* and *breaks* the loaves, and *gives* them to the disciples to share with the people. Jesus' table fellowship is for all who come (see Mark 6:30-44)!

Henri Nouwen helps us see that the disciples' attitude was one of fear. Jesus shifts the focus from fear and scarcity. Instead, Jesus helps the disciples see what they have (five loaves and two fish) as generous gifts from God which are to be gratefully shared. When we are controlled by fear, we are unable to be vehicles of God's gracious love. As Tilden Edwards said, "Grace at its simplest expresses the way life happens in faith: as an open, free gift, through and beyond and despite all we do."

Coming to the table to share *pan* is a central act of most

Christian communities. On Worldwide Communion Sunday in October, Christians are reminded that believers around the world are sharing Christ's body and blood in Eucharist from the rising of the sun to its setting all around the globe. They come to great cathedrals and to small one-room churches. They gather under trees and in grass huts; they sing in many different languages and eat many different kinds of bread. But, together with us, they are witnessing to the unity of God's church and to the amazingly diverse women, men, and children who are the body of Christ.

In an unforgettable passage, Augustine's insight continues to amaze the two of us:

> If you want to understand the body of Christ, listen to what the apostle Paul says to the faithful: 'You are the body of Christ, member for member' [see 1 Corinthians 12:27, Romans 12:5] You are Christ's own body, his members; thus, it is your own mystery which is placed on the Lord's table. It is your own mystery that you receive. For at communion, the priest says 'The body of Christ' and you reply 'Amen!' *When you say "Amen" you are saying yes to what you are.*
>
> (Sermon 272, italics ours)

When we receive the bread, we receive the mystery that our lives are part of one another. "We are *members one of another*" (Rom. 12:5). The "Amen" we pray is saying "So be it!" to our relationship with one another in Christ. We are not used to thinking of it that way! Augustine breaks open the meaning of scripture for us so that our participation at the Eucharist is given a new and vital dimension of sacramental meaning.

So it is that com-pan-ionship—community's sharing bread around the Table of Jesus Christ—becomes a central metaphor for those who seek to live sacramentally. Going to the communion rail at Epworth United Methodist Church in Chicago—with brothers and sisters who are black and white, brown and yellow, young and old, liberal and conservative, straight and gay, employed and unemployed, poor and well-to-do, bright and mentally-challenged—reminds us that at Jesus' Table there is only one prerequisite. By saying "yes" to God's invitation to accept the grace-filled promise that we are loved, we take our place at God's all-inclusive, justice-seeking Table.

One cannot be a solo Christian, for to be Christian is to be a member of the body of Christ. As scripture says:

> There is one body and one Spirit, just as you were called to the one hope of your calling, one Lord, one faith, one baptism, one God and Father of all, who is above all and through all and in all. But each one of us was given grace according to the measure of Christ's gift. . . . The gifts he gave were that some would be apostles, some prophets, some evangelists, some pastors and teachers, to equip the saints for the work of ministry, for building up the body of Christ, until all of us come to the unity of the faith and of the knowledge of the Son of God, to maturity, to the measure of the full stature of Christ. We must no longer be children, tossed to and fro and blown about by every wind of doctrine, by people's trickery, by their craftiness in deceitful scheming. But speaking the truth in love, we must grow up in every way into him who is the head, into Christ, from whom the whole body, joined and knit together by every ligament with which it is equipped, as each part is working properly, promotes the body's growth in building itself up in love.

> (Eph. 4:4, 6, 11-16)

From the day of the Church's birth at Pentecost until this day, we are bound together with brothers and sisters who claim the name and identity which Christ offers. Like all families, there are squabbles and sometimes, irrevocable breaks. But to be Christian is to be a part of Christ's body and to work, pray, and share at Table with those we like and with those we don't like. It is to live and love so that the fruits of the Spirit in our lives will be testimony to our membership in Christ's body. As the apostle Paul asserts: "The fruit of the Spirit is love, joy, peace, patience, kindness, generosity, faithfulness, gentleness, and self-control. . . . If we live by the Spirit, let us also be guided by the Spirit" (Gal. 5:22-23, 25).

Jesus reminded his hearers of that motley group of Hebrew slaves whom Moses had led across the Red Sea toward freedom. Then he went on to say, "I am the bread of life. Whoever comes to me will never be hungry" (John 6:35). God's gift of Jesus Christ offers living bread that came down from heaven to all who will receive it (see John 6:22-59).

One of the joys of spending our sabbatical at the Ecumenical Institute is that we are able to listen, dialogue, and pray with persons from many different backgrounds, experiences, parts of the world. Matt and Anne lead us in a pentecostal service reflecting their experiences in their homeland, Finland, and in Thailand where they have served as missionaries. Eugene leads us in a service based on the Reformed Church tradition as he has experienced it in his home in South Africa. Delrio prays with the deep intensity and spiritual fervor of the African-American experience. Kathleen combines patterns from her life in a Roman Catholic religious order with the spirituality of women in the church today. Tom leads a love feast out of the Wesleyan tradition. Each of our journeys are enriched as we experience traditions of worship different from our own.

We share and learn and pray together—Evangelical, Reformed, Pentecostal, Lutheran, United Methodist, Roman Catholic, Presbyterian. Often we are able to come to the Table together. When we are not, we are reminded of the brokenness and the pain that we must all work to heal. Christ's body, the Church, is called to embrace all nations and all peoples within God's arms of justice-love.

Recognizing that we are one body in Christ connects us with those we do not know. They feast at Christ's banquet table with many different rituals and in a multitude of places we have never been and may never be, but we are brothers and sisters in the Body of Christ. The One who binds us (Jesus Christ) is stronger than our differences.

Marcus Borg's provocative book, *Meeting Jesus Again for the First Time*, asserts that our images of Jesus are at the heart of our faith journeys. Our Christian life is linked with the images out of which we live. Many people have never moved beyond their childhood images of Jesus. They either judge them to be irrelevant and so give them lip service at best, or they hold them tenaciously while compartmentalizing religion from the more complex and informed areas of life.

Borg invites us to open ourselves to what Abraham Heschel calls "radical amazement"—moments when we are able to move beyond seeing something as "an intellectual paradox" and enter into "an experience of sacred mystery." When we bring our whole selves and walk into the holy, connections are made, and we are able to experience God in our day-to-day activities and experiences.

When Borg dared to do this, he came face-to-face with the post-Easter Jesus. Suddenly, the academic quest for the historical Jesus gave way to an awareness of the reality that the post-Easter Jesus gave the early church. This offers to us a light out of darkness and nourishment for our journeys from death to life. He invites others to move beyond doctrines and beliefs about God and into a life-giving relationship with God through Jesus Christ.

We need to take seriously our oneness with all those who accept Jesus' invitation to the Table. Doing this calls us to re-examine our own understandings of and experiences with our Host. Who is this Jesus Christ whose body we are?

When we reflect on those Jesus invited to the table, we cannot avoid the fact that he ate with tax collectors and sinners. He ate with women and others who were dispossessed. He was continually getting in trouble over those with whom he sat at table, for he did not always follow the ritual laws of his day. He shook his disciples to the core when he insisted on washing their feet before their last supper together.

As Christ's body, who are we to include and exclude? What religious laws and practices are we insisting on that become roadblocks instead of means of grace? Whose feet are we called to wash? And if this is to be for us a metaphor for servant ministry, whose servants are we to be and how are we to serve? Facing these questions will not allow us to hang onto our childish understandings! They bring us face to face with the One whose body we are.

When we claim that we are "members one of another" and are all an embodiment of Christ, we realize that we are all called to be "the salt of the earth" and "the light of the world" (Matt. 5:13-14). The post-Easter Jesus calls us to a task—not to a place of privilege.

As Christians, we need to remember that to be angry with our brothers or sisters or to insult them jeopardizes our place at the table (see Matthew 5:21-26). To be one with Christ means that we are called to be one with all Christians. And whenever we are tempted to draw lines which make us insiders and place others who claim Christ's name on the outside, we run the risk of receiving the same reprimand Jesus gave to the Pharisees of his day.

As Henri Nouwen reminds us in *Here and Now*: "God has given us to each other to build a community of mutual love where we can discover together that joy is not just for others but for all of us." We are recipients of this great sacramental gift when we dare to embrace all who are members of Christ's body, the Church.

Being bound to those we do not know because we break bread with One who breaks bread with them, calls us to a new humility. We must be open to the falling stars that surprise us as we listen with ears that hear and look with eyes that see! We will most certainly find ourselves coloring outside the lines of the ways we've always done things and the words we've always used! We discover that God is to be found in the unfamiliar as well as in the familiar. These brothers and sisters whom we have not met may show us what it means to follow Jesus if we will dare to remain open to their witness and ways.

CHAPTER SIX

Living into an Ecology of the Holy:

JOURNEY

Recently, at the rehearsal dinner for Jennifer and Joshua's wedding, we were talking with the bride's mother, Barbara. She asked us about our sabbatical plans, and we got into a great discussion about what it means to live sacramentally. Barbara said, "I think I had an experience like that." And she proceeded to share this story.

After Jennie was born, she had three miscarriages. It was devastating for this young family. Barbara began seeking help at a fertility clinic and then, once she conceived again, at an at-risk pregnancy clinic. "Everything about that pregnancy, Emily's birth and infancy, was super-charged with meaning for me," she said. She was pregnant in the springtime and "heavy with child" at Christmas!

Barbara described her sacramental experience. "It was early June. I took Jennie and Emily to the nearby park for a picnic and a chance to play on the grass. After lunch, I lay back on the blanket and held the baby up to the sky just to make her laugh. At that moment, I saw that the vast blue-ness of the cloudless sky was exactly the same shade of blue as Emily's eyes! I was just filled with an amazing sense of oneness with God. The vast goodness of God's creation was there, present in my little child. I knew God was holding us in God's hand."

She acknowledged what I heard in her voice and saw in her eyes. This memory still evokes the same intense emotion she experienced in that park as she lay on a blanket looking into her daughter's face twenty years before.

For Barbara, the present moment involved being a gracious host at the rehearsal dinner in the fellowship hall of her church the night before her elder daughter's wedding. But as we shared a meal together, she told us her story. The story wove together memories and hope, loss and gift, a baby daughter and a gracious God, and a grown daughter who was about to create a new family with her own hopes and dreams. It encompassed the faith community that helped her through the times of deep loss and was serving the meal at this time of joy.

In the telling of her story, Barbara became a weaver, creating a matrix of meaning. She shared the colors and emotions, the hopes and fears, the losses and the unspeakable gifts of a beautiful baby whose eyes became one with the sky. In her sharing, she embodied the deep knowing that in everything God holds us all in arms of love and compassion.

Sacramental living invites us into an ecology of the holy. Recognizing the holy particular in the objects of everyday living, sensing sacred space in both expected and unexpected places, kindling the fire with story and ritual, weaving the fabric of time and eternity, and receiving the grace of companions on our journey cannot be separated. They occur within a dynamic matrix, each influencing the others and being influenced by them.

The literal meaning behind the word ecology is "study of the house." It refers to the relationships between everything and everybody in the house and their environments—physical, historical, relational, spiritual and all the rest of the contexts in which we live. In this house of sacramental living, everything is important; nothing is inconsequential. Everything is in relation to everything else.

Richard Bresnahan, master potter and artist in residence at Saint John's, was showing us "Johanna." Johanna is the eighty-seven foot-long, three-chambered, wood-burning kiln he built to reflect his commitment to sustainable/renewable/indigenous art. He was musing on the interconnectedness of the universe. An astro-physicist who visited the kiln observed that what happens with the oxygen and hydrogen clouds in the kiln mirrors the birthing of stars and planets in the galaxy. Richard reminded us of Buckminster Fuller's observation that every action has not only a result, but also unknown resultants.

He was introduced to a clay deposit near Saint John's which would be disposed of because it was in the way of a road project. This deposit could provide clay for seven generations of potters—three hundred years. Yet, Richard knew banks would only be interested in a three- to five-year return. "If it isn't economically feasible in the short term, even valuable resources which took thousands of years to develop are seen as expendable waste to get rid of. What bank would give me a loan to buy and store three hundred years of clay?" he asked.

But Benedictines believe in the long view. For them, thinking in terms of three hundred years is not unreasonable. Their vow of stability connects them to the land and its total ecology. The clay is part of an ecology of the holy in which they seek to live. As Baldwin W. Dworschak (abbot, 1950-1971) writes about Saint John's:

> To have a sense of place is to lay claim to a place, not merely of possession, but more so of responsibility; this transforms simple ownership into reality. Whatever I see in this place calls me to account. It may rebuke me for neglecting its mes-

sage: this is a holy place, a friendly place, a place of hospitality, a place of prayer, of peace, a place of final preparation for eternity. This is a place of healing, of growth, of reconciliation, of natural beauty, of silence, and all this is sacramental.[1]

In the context of such a perspective, it is not surprising that Richard was authorized to purchase and move 18,000 tons of clay to stockpile on the abbey grounds.

The creations of Richard and his apprentices are made from that indigenous clay. Glazed with natural materials such as navy bean straw ash and flax straw ash (which Richard says was "gifted from a family farm in North Dakota"), the firing is done with ecological sensitivity. As we stood beside Johanna, we could sense the interconnectedness of each pot and pitcher not only with their artistic creators but with the whole universe.

We cannot attend to all things at once on a conscious level, but at the level of experiencing, this rich and complex matrix provides an inexhaustible reservoir for sacramental life. Whatever the icon we experience—whether a particular thing, place, story, event, or relationship—the doorway opens on the sacred and invites us to enter. Because sacrament is based on the experience of God's grace, we can be drawn in through that experience to the gifts made known through other icons as well. Indeed, we are able to apprehend the holy through a particular doorway because of other doorways we entered.

Think about basic and uncomplicated things such as fire, story, water, and food. Nathan Mitchell says we find in them roots of our human experience. When our ancestors traveled long ago they took fire, water, food and story with them. These are what nourished, sustained, and gave them their identity.

In our community worship we "gather the folks, sing the songs, tell the Story, and break the bread." Worship that does these things with vitality and integrity has deep meaning. But in both the list of what our ancestors needed, and the list of what worship involves, something is missing.

We got an important clue to this missing ingredient while driving to Chicago last weekend. We were reading Kenneth Grahame's *Wind in the Willows* aloud to each other. We had come to our favorite chapter—"The Piper at the Gates of Dawn." Rat and Mole encounter the mysterious Friend and Helper whose indescribable music has drawn them into his presence. They know this is a holy place. They experience, on the one hand, that they cannot ever again be afraid of One who calls forth unspeakable love from them. Yet, at the same time, their sense of awe is so deep that they also know something akin to fear. It is this sense of the Holy that is too often missing.

We begin with a particular thing or event; it is both unique and connected. In the "house of sacramental living," sensing the holy in and through the particular is essential. The translucence of these events or objects allows us to experience the presence of the holy. Such moments come and go in life. Rituals help us remember and relive the transforming power of these experiences.

Rituals that have life invite us into deep experiences through symbols that "sing in many voices." A symbol does not have one meaning. A symbol has a whole matrix of meanings. These meanings resonate not only with one another, but they also set up sympathetic vibrations with other symbols. Sacred stories do the same thing as they collide and dance with the meanings of other stories and symbols. Ritual gathers these together and embodies them within an ecology of the holy.

Such an ecology is wider and deeper than ritual. It is certainly not restricted to ritual. In ritual, however, the interconnections woven into such an ecology can be experienced if we have eyes to see and ears to hear. Even when we are not conscious of all that is present in such a context, we are affected at deep and profound levels.

When we began to think of the ritual where we experience that ecology most comprehensively, we agreed that for both of us, it is found in the great Vigil of Easter. Some of you have not experienced an Easter Vigil; sacramental living is not dependent on having done so! In it, however, we believe Christians may find insight into the ecology of the holy."

Robert Brooks says the Easter Vigil includes asking the question, "What is the Church saying to us about who we are?" If Lent says, "Become!" he believes Easter is saying, "You are!" In the Vigil, the Church invites us to experience these calls to faithful living by bringing together "an inexhaustible supply of symbols colliding upon one another." Here we find those elements Nathan Mitchell pointed to as basic for human experience: fire, story, water, and food.

These symbols and stories intersect and resonate. They combine to provide a matrix of meanings that tells us who we are as human beings and as the Church. They also say much about our relationship with God. The Vigil calls us into the presence of the holy that is above and beyond us, as well as among and within us.

Over and over again, we experience through story, symbol, and ritual acts the challenge: "This is who we are. Here is the loving, saving, holy Presence who calls, frees, nourishes, sustains, and empowers us. Has that good news grasped you yet? Here it is again. Listen! Attend! Participate!"

We gather, as our ancestors did, around the fire to hear the story, affirm our identity, and share the feast. Through many levels of meaning, our beliefs about who we are and about God are generated, experienced, and affirmed. We participate in the sacred stories that bind us to one another and reorient us to the future. We are challenged to join that great company of saints—past, present, and future—who journey from darkness to light, from bondage to freedom, from death to resurrection, and from mystery to ministry.

As the Easter Vigil begins, we gather in darkness. Darkness is an experiential metaphor for not being able to see. It symbolizes being unable to discern signs given to guide our journey. What the eyes of a seeing person cannot see in the darkness is paralleled by what a blind person cannot hear or touch or smell. Darkness stands for the experience of not being able to sense and discern what is around us.

Michael Naranjo, blinded by a hand grenade in Vietnam, describes how he "saw" Michelangelo's *David* with his fingers. We stood before that eighteen-foot sculpture in Florence and saw it with our eyes. But it becomes obvious as we watch the PBS video of Michael's experience, that he saw much more with his fingers than we were able to see with our eyes. Seeing in the Biblical sense is a deep knowing that comes through all of our senses. It comes from attending to and opening ourselves so that we are able to receive and experience.

Darkness, too, becomes a metaphor for being unable to see clearly. A person can be standing in a bright room and be unable to know what they see because they are imprisoned by their own blinders. As long as we can only see what we know, we remain in the dark.

When our children were young, we toured Jewel Cave in the Black Hills of South Dakota. At one point on the tour, as we are standing in a cavernous room deep underground, the park ranger tells us to stand still while he turns off all the lights. Being in total darkness is an awesome experience. The ranger asks us to put a hand in front of our face. Now we understand what it means to say, "I can't see my own hand in front of my face." When we are unable to be in relationship with our environment, we lose our sense of direction.

The physical experience of darkness reminds us of spiritual experiences, too. In the midst of deep struggles or depression, people talk about the "dark night of the soul." We are talking about more than our eyes when we sing I "was blind, but now I see," and when we affirm "the light of the world is Jesus."

In this darkness, a new fire is kindled, even as Patrick kindled it on the Hill of Slane so many years ago. When Christian communities begin the Easter Vigil in darkness and kindle the new fire, we are ritualizing a basic human truth. When the park ranger in Jewel Cave throws the switch and light floods that cavernous room, we know what a great gift light is!

The writer of First John proclaims "that God is light, and in [God] there is no darkness at all" (1 John 1:5). Both Isaiah and Matthew proclaim:

The people who sat in darkness
    have seen a great light,
and for those who sat in the region and
        shadow of death,
    light has dawned.
                    (Isa. 9:1-2; Matt. 4:16)

The Easter Vigil is only one of many places where Christians are reminded that Christ is the light of the world.

From the new fire, the great paschal candle is lit. It is sign and symbol of the resurrection. In the darkness of the tomb, the light of the risen Christ shines forth. "Light of Christ," we hear. "Thanks be to God," we sing in response. In some celebrations of the Vigil, members of the community light individual candles from the paschal candle. The light of the resurrection is not confined; it is to shine in the lives of an Easter people. "You are the light of the world," Matthew's Gospel says. "A city built on a hill cannot be hid. No one after lighting a lamp puts it under the bushel basket, but on the lampstand, and it gives light to all in the house. In the same way, let your light shine before others, so that they may see your good works and give glory to your Father in heaven" (Matt. 5:14-16). It is not enough to be grateful for the gift of light. We are called to be the light in our dark and hurting world. Gift brings responsibility!

The service of light at the great Vigil of Easter resonates with our use of light at other times too. We light candles on the Lord's Table each Sunday as the community gathers for worship. In many congregations, the acolytes take the light from the candles before extinguishing them at the close of the service, so that they can lead the people out into the world with the light of Christ preceding them.

During Advent, we light first one candle and then two, three, and four—as we move closer to the celebration of Christmas. At our Christmas eve services, we add to the four candles, the light from the Christ candle.

Linda often creates a visual center for some of her classes. She reminds her students that we light candles in our worship, to remind us of the Spirit's presence. When we light a candle in our classroom, we are reminding ourselves that the Spirit is present here as well. That reminder makes a difference in the ways we listen and speak to one another.

Sometimes at Christian weddings, a unity candle is lit—symbolizing the creating of a new family. Once we watched the parents of the bride and groom light the candles on each side of the unity candle. The bride and groom then used these candles to light the unity candle. These candles represented each of their families.

Light is a powerful symbol. We need to think carefully about when and how we use it so that it speaks what we mean to affirm. We are always a little disconcerted when a bride and groom light the unity candle and then blow out their individual (or family) candles. After all, they are bringing who they are into the marriage; their lives as individuals are not being snuffed out!

In Jewish homes, the mother lights the candles for Shabbat on Friday evenings. Those gathered remember all God has done and continues to do for them. Christians, too, can use candles as we gather around our tables for family meals and for meals with friends in ways that are more than aesthetic. As we light them, we can pray: "Blessed are you, Creator God, for you bring forth light from darkness; shine within and among us as we break bread and share community with one another today." Often we invite our guests to sing with us one line of a hymn as a response: "Now thank we all our God, with heart and hands and voices."

Whenever we connect birthday candles with God's gift of life and growth, we are enriching a cultural and family ritual by connecting it with our own growth "in wisdom and in years, and in divine and human favor" (Luke 2:52). These simple acts become a part of the matrix for sacramental living.

As the community enters the darkened church following the light of the paschal candle for the Easter Vigil, light overcomes darkness. Three times the procession pauses to hear "Light of Christ" and sing in response, "Thanks be to God!"

Then we hear the *Exsultet*, that great Easter song of proclamation which tradition decrees be used only at this service, which concludes:

Accept this Easter candle,
a flame divided but undimmed,
a pillar of fire that glows to your honor.

Let it mingle with the lights of heaven,
and continue bravely burning to dispel the darkness of
the night!
May the Morning Star, which never sets,
find this flame still burning:
Christ, that Morning Star, who
came back from the dead,
and shed his peaceful light on all creation,
your Son who reigns for ever and ever! Amen.[2]

Fire and light are symbols that call forth many layers of meaning in an ecology of the holy. Their meaning is clarified and enriched as we encounter them again and again in the sacred stories we share.

Robert Brooks reminds us that the nine scripture readings in the Easter Vigil tell us who and Whose we are and what we are becoming. It is "an intensive, mini-course in salvation history."

Salvation history isn't quick and easy. It starts with creation. Hearing the nine scriptures takes a long time. Often we get tired. The first time we experienced all these readings, we thought they were too long and there were too many of them. Then we learned the service used to take all night. Now this two-hour service is one we anticipate with joy!

Attendance at the Easter Vigil at St. Luke's grew each year as folks learned to love this service. Our students report similar experiences in parishes they serve. As we noted earlier, there is no other time when Christians hear the sweep of this great story in all its power in a single service.

Gradually we have recognized that the story proclaimed is really our own story—not simply because it is the story of "my people," but because it rehearses the everyday experiences of our lives. We have known times of chaos when the Spirit of

God moved on the face of the waters. We have rejoiced when God said, "Let there be light," in the dark nights of our souls. We have been overwhelmed with the flood, adrift without a rudder, held up only by the ark of the Church; and we have been given the rainbow sign in surprising times and places.

We have been enslaved by our own desires, by the expectations and conditioning of our families and our culture. These powers of this world can overwhelm us but we have also been led through the waters of baptism to freedom. There we discover we need nourishment and direction as we wander in the wilderness on our way with fellow pilgrims headed toward the promised land.

We have seen the valley full of dry bones—the moribund rigidity of a church when it fails to claim that new life in Jesus Christ is open to all. But we have also been richly blessed as the breath of the Spirit blows new life into the Church in unexpected ways. Oh, yes, this is our story! This is your story too. This is the story of all the Church—of all who say "yes" to the invitation to be a part of the body whose head is Jesus Christ.

By knowing sacred stories, we can find points of intersection with our own stories. Even familiar stories can grasp us in surprising ways. That happened to Dwight when he was pastor at St. Luke's. Linda had been called to serve on the faculty at Garrett-Evangelical. Although we discerned through prayer and counsel with others that she needed to answer that call, nothing seemed to be available for Dwight. So, although we had often said that we would never consider a commuter marriage, we found ourselves in one!

Dwight was on his monthly "desert day"—a time of quiet, prayer, and meditation on scripture. The question of what he should do in the future was not in the forefront of his mind that day, although it was always simmering on a back burner. He was reading the story of Saul's conversion. Suddenly, one sentence leapt from the page and burned itself into his consciousness: "Go into the city, and there it will be told you what you are to do" (cf. Acts 9:6, AP).

Nothing about assurances, or guarantees, or knowing in advance what the outcome would be for a white, fifty-year-old male. There was further conversation, prayer, and discernment to test out the revelation/insight. But from that time on, the trajectory of decision-making proceeded in a different direction. Into the city he went! Although it took nearly three years for a full time vocational setting to evolve, he never doubted that this was indeed a "word from the Lord."

His assurance came from the inner conviction that as he read the story of Saul, God's Spirit reached through the story, grasped his attention, and God's Spirit bore witness with his spirit that calling involves risk and faith. Stories can carry us on our faith journeys.

We do not read the Bible in a vacuum. We come with our own problems and questions, joys, and sorrows. We each bring our own contexts when we read and hear the Word. We also hear it as a community of God's people with our corporate concerns and experiences. That is part of our context as well.

The setting makes a difference, too, in how we hear the Story. We hear the readings of the Vigil in other circumstances, but here they are heard within the context of a celebration of the Resurrection. The Easter candle illumines what we hear; everything is seen in light of the cross and the empty tomb! The stories take on new meaning because "Christ is risen!"

Creation is linked with the new creation, light out of darkness with the Light of Christ, the waters of the flood with the waters of baptism, the Exodus with the Resurrection. In the silence, through the prayers, and with the hymns we sing, many layers of meaning are woven together. In faith we sing:

Come, ye faithful, raise the strain of
triumphant gladness;
God hath brought forth Israel into joy from sadness;
loosed from Pharaoh's bitter yoke
Jacob's sons and daughters,
led them with unmoistened foot
through the Red Sea waters.

'Tis the spring of souls today;
Christ hath burst his prison,
and from three days' sleep in death
as a sun hath risen;
all the winter of our sins,
long and dark, is flying
from his light, to whom we give
laud and praise undying.[3]

With many symbols and images weaving and pulsing like the northern lights in our experience, the sacred stories of our worshiping community carry us from fire to font.

The paschal candle first lit at the Easter Vigil goes with us throughout the church year. It will give forth its light at all our services of worship during the great fifty days from Easter to Pentecost. We light the paschal candle at funeral services as we celebrate the death and resurrection of those who die.

What a powerful experience it was for us to enter the Abbey Church at Saint John's and to see the paschal candle burning brightly beside the open wooden casket of one of the monks. Father Jude had spent more than sixty years ministering in Christ's name. Many years of that ministry were spent among Native Americans. As we joined the monks in morning and midday prayers, the silent resurrection witness of the paschal candle burned brightly.

The celebration of the baptismal covenant comes after the Service of the Word in the Easter Vigil. For the New Testament writers, death and resurrection are at the heart of baptism. Within the context of the Great Vigil, that connection cannot be ignored. The use of the paschal candle (which is also called the Easter candle) at all services celebrating the baptismal covenant reminds us of this connection.

The "prayer over the water" proclaims that Christ called his disciples "to share in the baptism of his death and resurrection, and to make disciples of all nations." We pray for the Holy Spirit to be poured out so that dying and being raised with Christ, the baptized may share in his final victory.

This prayer proclaims again what we have just heard in the readings: creation out of chaos, light out of darkness, the rainbow sign after the flood, freedom out of slavery—all stories where the image of water plays an important part.

Do we know, yet, who we are and Whose we are called to be? Has baptism claimed us so that it is not only a ritual event, but becomes the mark of our ongoing discipleship? For this service is not only for those being baptized; it is for all who have been baptized too.

In the vows of the baptismal covenant, we renounce "the spiritual forces of wickedness, reject the evil powers of this world, and repent of [our] sin" once again. We "accept the freedom and power God gives [us] to resist evil, injustice, and oppression in whatever forms they present themselves." And we "confess Jesus Christ as [our] Savior, put [our] whole trust in his grace, and promise to serve him as [our] Lord." That's what it's all about!

At a Greek Orthodox service Linda attended, as members went forward to receive the bread and wine, those with newly baptized babies also carried the baby's lighted baptismal candle as a symbol of the new life which baptism brings. That ritual act reminds participants of the connection between the light and the gift of new life through water and the Spirit. The fire of the Spirit and the sacred stories carry us to the font.

Sacramental living is our embodying the truths behind the baptismal vows we affirm at the Easter Vigil each year. We are called to reflect on and reaffirm them every time we are present at a baptism. Baptism commissions us to ministry in Christ's name. It is our ordination to the priesthood of all believers. That priesthood is reaffirmed as we receive the laying on of hands and hear the words: "The Holy Spirit work within you, that having been born of water and the Spirit, you may live as a faithful disciple of Jesus Christ."

Linda had a conversation with a colleague and friend who was struggling to make a decision about seeking ordination as an elder. The conversation revolved around what it means to "put our whole trust in God's grace." Having prepared herself for ministry, is she now called to serve as a licensed local pastor or should she continue in the process for ordination as elder? This is not always easy or even clear as we live in the midst of the tensions and pressures of politics in our denominational lives. One's faithfulness is tested in the process of discerning; there is no one right path for all Christians.

A United Methodist pastor was suspended recently by his bishop because he performed a covenant service for two women in his congregation. He acted on what he discerned to be "the freedom and power God gives to resist evil, injustice, and oppression." He acted with a pastor's heart, knowing that there could be consequences. The bishop, on the other hand, acted on his vows to uphold the Discipline of the church. Both sought to act faithfully to God and to their vows.

Christians will not always agree on what God requires of them. Peter and Paul did not always agree either. The issue is not that all Christians agree. Rather, the issue is for each person to seek to live as faithfully as he or she can within the context of his or her faith community. Acting in faith and accepting the consequences for our acts is what we are called to do.

The Good News of the Gospel is that God will receive our faithful acts and use them for good—even when we make mistakes. Sin is not taking seriously the vows that we made or being persuaded to act for political or economic reasons rather than accepting what God is asking of us.

As Christians, we are called to recognize the rainbow signs God gifts us with each day. God calls us toward including rather than excluding, toward compassion rather than self-righteousness judgment, and toward freedom for all rather than privilege for a few. Our baptism calls us to compassion and companionship, not privilege and privatism. In an ecology of the holy, ritual is not restricted to a separated sacred time and place. Baptism marks us with an identity that interpenetrates all we are and everything we do.

When Dwight's Dad died, all three of our children returned for their grandfather's funeral. When we called our eldest son Mark in Boston three weeks later to tell him of Grandma Vogel's death, he said, "If Dad needs me to come again, I will." On the spur of the moment, Dwight said, "Tell Mark that what I'd like most of all would be for all our family to be together next Thanksgiving." He and his wife Virginia said they would come.

The following Thanksgiving, they joined our other two children and their families at our home in Chicago. Three generations gathered around the dining room table. For the first time, we realized we are now the elders of the tribe. We are entrusted with the family stories and tradition. We can no longer say, "Let's ask Grandpa or Grandma!"

On one level, what we did was quite ordinary. We lit the candles and prayed together. We ate the traditional Thanksgiving foods. We told stories that connected us with earlier generations. We affirmed our identity as a family. We laughed and cried together.

On another level, none of this was ordinary at all. Because of the recent deaths of Dwight's parents, this first Thanksgiving marked a transition in the family. The old had passed away; something new had come. Everything we said and did had a new level of meaning. We parted, knowing we were bound together in spite of distances, facing a future that would be different from the past. The feast was a ritual of endings and new beginnings. As Goethe says in *Faust*, "What you have received as heritage from your ancestors now take as task, so as to make it your own."

We see this as the Easter Vigil moves from Light through Word and Water to Feast. It does not leave the experience of previous parts of the service behind. Rather it gathers them up and propels them forward. In the Easter Eucharist, all we have done is present, symbol upon symbol, experience upon experience, memory upon memory, life experience upon life experience.

Here is holy particularity: bread and cup resonate with water and flame. Here is sacred space (for the feast itself consecrates any space in which it is celebrated). We find ourselves positioned before the empty tomb. Here the story of Jesus eating with his disciples is told again as we reach back to claim and appropriate the readings we heard of the Last Supper. We reach forward to the post-resurrection breaking of bread at Emmaus, and Jesus' breakfast with the disciples beside the sea. Here ritual and story kindle the fire of the Spirit in our hearts.

Here past, present, and future are woven together. We recall the story of the Last Supper but Easter Eucharist is not its re-enactment. It is the celebration that the Risen Christ is with us in the present. "Thy kingdom come" we pray, and the future of God's rule and reign invades that present moment and transforms it.

Here we are literally companions, for we break bread together—not only with our friends and the people we happen to like. For if we are children of God, we have as our brothers and sisters all those in God's family.

Jesus was frequently in trouble because he insisted on having table fellowship with those whom others wanted to exclude. We believe that the Table to which Jesus Christ invites us offers a means of grace to all who respond to this invitation with sincerity. Jesus Christ is the Host, and we come with all God's children to be fed.

Often it is easier to open ourselves to the mystery of the Holy One, awesome as that is, than to open ourselves to the companions around us. But if we accept Jesus' invitation to come, we will eat with those whom our culture labels "outcasts and sinners."

This is the mystery we receive: the bread we break is a sharing in the body of Christ, and we are that body, members one of another. Often we do not realize that it is our own life story we rehearse in this great ritual.

One of our students found a way to make that come alive in life transforming ways. David Burkette took on a major final project for one of Linda's classes. He designed a retreat for those who had experienced the loss of a loved one some months before and who felt ready to come together with others to share their grief and to walk into new life. The setting for this retreat is the church, and it begins on Holy Thursday and ends on Easter morning.

Participants come together to share their stories, to grieve, and to pray. But they also have important tasks to do. They prepare the sacred space for the services that take place during these holy days. They participate in the Thursday evening Tenebrae service, serving as acolytes who extinguish the candles as the sanctuary grows darker and darker. They strip the altar in preparation for the Good Friday service. They drape the cross in black. They carry the Christ candle out of the darkened church at the end of the service. They read the scriptures and lead in the prayers at the Good Friday service. They toll the bell.

After each of these services, they reflect together on how the story of Christ's death and these liturgical acts connect with their own experiences of death and loss. They study scripture; they pray; they cry. They become a community—supporting one another and listening with grace and care.

On Saturday, they bake the bread for the Easter Vigil. They talk about the role of yeast. They punch the dough down; they watch it rise. They savor the aroma of bread baking in the oven. Then they get things ready for the kindling of the new fire and for the procession from darkness to light. They prepare the space for the highest festival of the church year. They share in reading the lessons in the service. They renew their own baptismal vows as a group. They serve as eucharistic ministers as the congregation celebrates the feast around the Table.

Before the Easter morning services, they arrange the lilies they and others have given in memory of those saints of the church who have died. Together they celebrate the healing that has occurred and will continue to occur in them as they affirm to one another, "Christ is risen!" "Christ is risen indeed!"

The Easter Eucharist is a great mystery. We never exhaust its meaning. In it, we proclaim the paschal mystery in word and act through sign, symbol and sacrament: "Christ has died! Christ is risen! Christ will come again!"

But this mystery calls us into ministry. Just as baptism commissions us for our ministry as Christians, eucharist feeds us with bread broken in sacred space so that we can feed the world. If Christ is "bread of the world, in mercy broken," and we are the body of Christ, then we must become bread for the world.

We will never forget the Eucharist where worshipers were invited to bring loaves of bread from their cultural, ethnic, or family traditions. One loaf was used for the celebration of the Eucharist and the rest were piled high in baskets at the foot of the Lord's Table. It was an amazing symbol of the rich diversity of the congregation. "This bread which we break, is it not a sharing in the body of Christ?" We heard the familiar words with new ears.

At fellowship time following the service, we shared bread and butter. What a wonderfully diverse and delicious array of textures, shapes, and tastes! Once more, we were reminded that we are the body of Christ. Families from the congregation took the remaining loaves to the community's soup kitchen and to a homeless shelter at a church in the city. The body of Christ is broken for you . . . and you . . . and you . . . and me. The Body of Christ, whose body we are, is given for the whole world!

The ecology of the holy is not something we achieve; it is a perspective we live into. It connects mystery with ministry, enabling us to sense the sacred, kindle the fire, weave the fabric, and break bread with companions as we live into the rich abundance of God's grace.

Notes
1. *A Sense of Place II: The Benedictines of Collegeville*, ed. Colman J. Barry, O.S.B. (Collegeville, Minn: The Liturgical Press, 1990), 75.

2. An excerpt from the English translation of *Exsultet* from *The Roman Missal*.

3. John of Damascus, trans. John Mason Neal, "Come, Ye Faithful, Raise the Strain," *The United Methodist Hymnal* (Nashville, Tenn: The United Methodist Publishing House, 1989), 315.

CHAPTER SEVEN

Embracing Mystery:

SACRAMENTAL LIVING

The evening of October 31 wasn't at all like the Halloweens of our childhood. Oh, there were jack-o-lanterns on porches and costumed trick-or-treaters who came to our door. But these are not what we treasure.

This year we celebrated the Vigil for the Feast of All Saints with the monks of Saint John's Abbey. With many other guests, we gathered with the monks in the dimly lit baptistry. A very tall and stark statue of John the Baptist towered over us. The paschal candle was burning beside the large baptismal font. We could hear its water gurgling softly.

Incense wafted about the room from a brazier in front of two large reliquaries that stood nearby. Reliquaries contain something connected with a saint: a bit of clothing, a strand of hair, a fragment of bone. Reliquaries are not a part of our tradition. In fact, as protestants we were warned of their potential for abuse. But at this service, these signs of the saints from the past connected us with the Church through the ages.

After the opening prayers and readings, we joined in the procession through the nave and up to the choir stalls around the Table. Throughout the darkened church, small reliquaries were placed on the top of many pew-backs, each with a votive candle burning beside it. There were also many candles around the sanctuary with nothing beside them. These candles reminded us of the many saints whose names we do not know—those who make up that great company of the unnamed faithful.

As we processed we heard a litany of the saints chanted: " . . . Saint John the Baptist . . . Saint Peter and Saint Paul . . . Saint Andrew . . . Saint Mary Magdalene . . . Saint Augustine . . . Saint Catherine of Siena" and so many more. Then to be certain none of the faithful saints are left out: "All holy men and women." And after each name, the congregation responded by singing "pray for us."

By the time all were gathered around the Table, we knew we were surrounded by "a great cloud of witnesses" (Heb. 12:1). We remembered those we hold close in our hearts—Lena, Marvin, Henry, Grace, Sophia.

The chanting of the psalms was beautiful, as it always is. After Abbot Timothy read the Gospel, the bells in the great bell banner outside the church began to ring—first one, then another, until all five were pulsing with sound. We became aware that the organ had started to play, first softly, then more and more vibrantly until the stalls (and the people in them) began to vibrate with the music and the bells.

We sang the *Te Deum* and as we did, the abbot poured incense onto the burning coals in the thurible, and smoke began to rise. This symbol reaches all the way back to Old Testament practices. When Isaiah came into the presence of the Holy God, "the house was filled with smoke" (Isa. 6:4). The incense is a sign of the presence of the Spirit of God that "blows where it chooses" (John 3:8); its path cannot be controlled and it penetrates everything!

First the Abbot circled the Table, swinging the censer as the smoke of the incense rose—we felt the Spirit of God as the incense filled that space. Then the abbot swung the censer out over the reliquaries and those candles of the unnamed faithful flickering throughout the nave. We remembered that the Spirit of God is present in their witness in prayer, word, and deed. We experienced what it means when we say in the Apostles' Creed: "We believe . . . in the communion of saints."

And then Abbott Timothy moved slowly, circling the congregation. Oh, how great the mystery! The Spirit of God is present among my brothers and sisters here! We bowed our heads as the incense passed by. Wonder of wonders, we were filled with awe as the Spirit (symbolized by the incense) also fell upon us.

With candles burning, bells ringing, the organ playing, incense wafting, and people singing, we were transported into the presence of the Holy One. We experienced the Truth that, by God's grace, the Holy is beyond, within, and among us. As we looked at each other, we recognized how seldom we are ushered into this great sense of Mystery.

Put alongside that marvelous liturgical experience, another very different experience of the Holy. Standing beside the atmospheric chamber of the giant kiln at Saint John's, Richard Bresnahan recalled something he learned from an elderly Japanese potter: "Folks worry about where the pots are. The secret of the firing is where the pots are not." Richard pointed to the large empty chamber: "The empty space here determines what happens when you fire the pots. A Benedictine brother who helped build the heating plant here taught me that 'it is easier to pull the flame than to push the flame!'"

Silence and solitude may appear to be empty spaces to the casual observer. Yet what happens there vitally effects our being and doing. Silence does not come naturally to Dwight. He had to learn to develop this shadow side of his being. Gradually he has learned the importance of that apparently empty space. There the fire of the Spirit can enable him to embrace Mystery, rather than trying to push the Spirit by doing more and more. We must take time to be or our doing becomes superficial.

We were walking home from Richard's studio and kiln when Linda said: "Let's take the footbridge path." It's about three times as far that way, and it comes from a part of the campus which is usually out of the way for us, but this evening it was near at hand. We walked down the trail and started across the little bridge.

The sight left us breathless. Over Little Lake Watab the mist was shimmering, the sun was setting, and the autumn trees and bushes were reflected in the water. What an incredible sight! We stood and marveled at such beauty. Signs of the Great Creator's work were present everywhere. The mist flowed around us and hovered close to the water. Once again, we were transported into the presence of the Spirit. The pale pink of the setting sun, the mist, the elusive reflection of the trees on the lake—it was as if we had walked into Monet's *Morning on the Seine*. We lived into that sacramental moment with wonder and thanksgiving.

When we got home, we called friends and our daughter to witness to the gift of God's presence we had experienced. Even when there are not words enough, it seems we are impelled to speak about all that we have seen. Mystery is an indispensable part of the sacramental. We have seen how the Greek word *mysterion* was translated in the Latin as *sacramentum*. The connection between the two concepts is deeply ingrained in our heritage.

Today's world is much more concerned with explanation and analysis than with appreciation and mystery. But even in a cultural context that often fails to value mystery, we are blessed when we open ourselves to the Mystery of God. These experiences are deeper than logical explanations. A scientific description of that sunset cannot capture the depth of our experience. A poem or musical composition may come closer, but even these do not exhaust the power and meaning of what we experience.

Gabriel Marcel's distinction between mysteries and problems is helpful here. We consider problems as objects to be studied, analyzed, and solved. A problem is "thrown in front of us." It is something apart from us. Thinking and acting in terms of problem solving is a useful and productive approach for mathematics and the physical sciences. However, the claim that it is the only approach is an oversimplification of experience.

Marcel contrasts problem with mystery. Mystery involves us in profound ways. There is a deep personal relationship with what we encounter as Mystery. Mysteries involve us at the very core of our being. Mystery does not stand over against us, but is a presence. Marcel notes that someone can be in the same room with us, but be an object, a "stranger." When that person is a stranger to me, I am also a stranger to myself.

When a person is a presence, my inner being is refreshed. I am not only in significant relationship with that person, but I become more fully myself. A mutual sense of presence makes us aware that we participate in a Mystery. Although we cannot fully articulate it, this mystery makes a difference to who we are.

Life lived at the surface is oblivious to mystery around us. Marcel notes that there are "presences" which we do not experience as *presence*. Indeed, he observes, they almost seem like part of the furniture. Yet, even on the surface, some pieces don't quite fit into the puzzle of life. Multiple levels of meaning lurk around the edges of our consciousness. Paths of sacramental living lead us beneath the surface to a sense of *real presence.* We are led to a deeper and more holistic appreciation and appropriation of life.

Sensing a presence means we become aware of the holy particularity that makes this thing, this event, or this person unique. Yet, the Mystery of that presence includes connections that resonate with other moments of presence. We are invited to embrace the Mystery. A creative tension plays between the unique and the way all things are connected. This opens the way for things, events, and companions to become translucent conveyors of grace. Whenever we are grasped by that sense of the sacred, the veil of ordinary experiencing is torn open. We *know* we are in the presence of Mystery.

What happens when these moments pass? Kenneth Grahame in *The Wind in the Willows* offers one answer. After Rat and Mole have experienced the mysterious, awesome presence of the great Friend and Helper, memory of the experience quickly fades. For Grahame, forgetfulness of the mysterious moment is a gift. Without forgetfulness, we would only yearn to relive it again, and that would make us miserable. We are left with only faint echoes, bits of the marvelous music. Even then, we do not grasp the meaning. For if the awe should continue, Grahame says, our "frolic" would turn to "fret."

We find Grahame's story beautiful and powerful, a favorite across the years. But we recognize that he is not describing a Christian experience of sacramental living. We, too, have deep and profound experiences of the presence of the great Friend and Helper whom we know in Jesus Christ. And beyond the temptation to turn God into a "buddy" always at our beck and call, we know that our God is holy, awesome Mystery. We can only keep silence or sing! For us, as for Rat and Mole, moments of mystery pass away, much as we try to hold onto them. But there the similarities stop.

Through things, place, story, symbol, ritual, and companions, we tend the memory of Mystery. In the tending, Mystery may become present to us again. Sometimes, in a special moment of grace, our rehearsing and re-membering leads us back into the presence of that Mystery. That is what the liturgy—the work of the people of God who meet in Christ's name—does for us.

Dwight remembers one particular Sunday morning at Calvary Church in Le Mars. He didn't feel like going to worship. If he hadn't been directing the choir and teaching a Sunday School class, he might not have gone. But he went (unwillingly, as John Wesley went to Aldersgate!). One of the songs in the service was one of Charles Albert Tindley's great African-American hymns, *Stand By Me*. Somehow God reached beyond Dwight's despair and apathy and brought him into the presence of the Holy One. It wasn't just a matter of feeling better; his perspective was transformed. He can't articulate it now any more than he could then, but he knows it made a difference.

Embracing mystery nurtures sacramental living. Experiences of mystery are means of grace where God meets us, by appointment as it were. But we must be open to receive the gift that is given. Too often, we don't look skyward, and we allow ourselves to be contained within the lines of habit and tradition. We remain unable to sense the sacred.

Odo Casel, writing in 1932, observed that modern persons thought they had driven "the darkness of Mystery" away. They could approach life in the light of reason, with the expectation that they could master everything. Already when he was writing, it was becoming clear that human beings were not in control as much as they thought they were. Even where that control was clearly exhibited, the results could be horrendous as depression and war made clear.

For Casel, the great mystery is the revelation of God in Christ, incarnate as a human being, who now becomes present to us through the mysteries of worship. With Saint Ambrose, Casel could say, "I find you in your mysteries." Mystery is basic to our religion, our spirituality, and our worship. He found mystery at the core of the liturgy in the saving work of the risen Christ.

When this is a *real presence*, as Marcel uses the term, we are related to that work at the depths of our being in life-transforming ways. We discover who we are. We become more fully who we are meant to be. We are united to Christ in the mystery of worship.

However, sometimes our rituals seem empty, the stories irrelevant, and the people around us become irritants or strangers. What, then?

Mystery is at the heart of the Christian faith. God is not made in our image, and that includes the image of our emotions. Just because I can't feel God when I pray doesn't mean God is not hearing my prayers. The good news is that God is with us even when all we can sense is God's absence. The Mystery is that God is Emmanuel (God-with-us) even when we are unaware of the Mystery. Sacramental living calls us to trust that God is greater than our experiences of God.

Linda experienced the awesome and mysterious One as she stood on that Canadian highway with our son safely in her arms. Her questions melted and she was given the gift of knowing with her heart that God's compassion and care surrounded her and her dying father and her son. Indeed, the whole world is in God's hands!

Sometimes when we hold a newborn baby in our arms or stand in the awesome presence of death, we are enveloped in God's awesome presence. Those who risk loving and being loved, are sometimes overwhelmed with the goodness of God.

Too often, as inheritors of the Enlightenment, we close ourselves to whatever defies our understanding. When we do this, we miss many of the gifts God offers us. But when we dare to open ourselves to sacramental living, surprises abound!

At other times, we allow fear that has been fostered in us in the name of "remaining faithful" to close us down. We are unable to experience God in the unfamiliar. Before Vatican II, many of our Roman Catholic friends feared they would loose their souls if they entered a protestant church. We grew up in churches that saw Roman Catholic devotional practices as superstitious and idolatrous. Instilling fear is often a tool used to control persons and keep them in line. Such tactics are not in keeping with the life and ministry of Jesus.

We arrived in Bangalore, India, on New Year's eve. Father David met us at the airport and took us to *Chaminad Niral* (the Marianist house). That evening we went to the chapel and sat on the floor on mats in a large circle around a low Lord's Table. One of the brothers entered carrying a bowl with a flaming wick. He made a small circle with the light, then a larger circle, and finally a large and expansive one. A lamp with seven wicks was lit in front of the Table. We sang Christian *bhajans* (spiritual songs). At midnight, with the sounds of firecrackers going off in the street outside, we ushered the new year in as we shared the Eucharist with joy and thanksgiving.

We sat around the dining room table afterwards, with welcoming garlands around our necks. We asked many questions as we shared with Father David and our new friends. We learned that the ritual of bringing in the flame is called *arati*, the "offering of lights." The first small circle signifies the presence of the Holy Spirit within us; the second circle is a sign of the presence of the Holy Spirit in the community; the largest circle reminds us of the presence of the Spirit in the whole world and beyond.

The magi who came to worship Jesus would not have found this ritual act strange. They were likely Zoroastrians whose worship centered on the light. In the starry heavens, they found signs of the ongoing war between light and darkness. That is why they followed the star. Zoroastrians brought their sense of the significance of light from Persia to India. There it resonated with tribal religious practices and Hindu worship. Like the bath of initiation (baptism) and the fellowship meal (Eucharist) and countless other symbols, the offering of light is a deeply symbolic practice shared by many religious traditions around the world.

Such symbols and practices are often 'baptized,' that is, placed within a Christian context and given meaning that resonates with the Christian story. Many of the symbols we use are not our private property; they are widely shared. We put the stamp of our religious tradition upon these symbols but that does not mean we own them or that our understanding is the only one. The mystery of the holy is inexhaustible!

Before we went to India, our colleague and friend Barbara Troxell introduced us to the writings of Abhishiktānanda (Henri le Saux). He was a Belgian Benedictine priest (1910–1973) who went to India to study Hinduism so that he could be more effective in sharing the Christian Story there. He developed a deep appreciation for Hindu spirituality, while remaining a faithful Roman Catholic centered in daily celebration of the Eucharist. In *Guru and Disciple*, Abhishiktānanda teaches us that no one may claim to have true knowledge of Christ until they realize that Christ's mystery is all embracing.

Abhishiktanānda describes in vivid detail the Hindu worshipers' ritual at "first light" as they stand in the river "waiting for the mystic hour." As day meets night and night meets day, Hindus express adoration and praise. Abhishiktānanda says, "Only those whose souls have remained totally insensitive to the mystery of the 'holy lights,' a mystery both inner and cosmic, and to this marvelous epiphany of God in . . . creation, would think of labeling such rites idolatrous." We believe this is true.

Our belief was soon put to the test when we found ourselves as guests of Swami Nityananda Giri (which means the joy of the unchanging) at the Hindu ashram and temple of Sri Gnanananda, who so influenced Abhishiktānanda. This temple is far off the tourist route in India. Father David met this swami at a meeting of the Abhishiktānanda Society. When David told the swami we were coming to India, he invited the three of us to be his guests.

This highly-educated, sensitive Hindu priest and teacher offered us warm hospitality. Some of our misconceptions about Hinduism were dispelled. We learned much we had not known. We found many similarities and many differences in our religious traditions. We are better Christians because we were blessed to encounter Hinduism through this swami.

As evening descended we observed people praying in their temple. Young boys, whose school we would visit the next morning, processed around the temple. A family from California had returned 'home' and with the grandparents shared in a Hindu ritual of blessing their new baby. There was music: drums and a double-reed pipe—lovely but strange to our ears. There were candles, flowers, sweets, and the ringing of bells. There were smells, sounds, and sights that almost created sensory overload; yet, it was very worshipful. There was a sense of reverence and inclusivity, personal piety and devotion.

Swami explained many things to us. Krishna's flute is empty (hollow) bamboo "so God's music can get in." We, too, must empty our minds to be in touch with ourselves (atman). Swami told stories and used humor to teach. His Advaitic

Hinduism is very meditative and inward though he believes it is important to offer folks access to the Holy at whatever "door" they are.

As we entered one area, we came upon a group of women lighting the seven-tiered evening lamp. Abhishiktānanda writes about a holy moment filled with the Mystery of the Divine Presence in the preface to *Guru and Disciple*: "There is no light anywhere which is not a reflection of the one eternal Light, in which all things were made and in whose radiance all . . . awaken to themselves. From every corner of the horizon the Spirit is calling to the Bride and Christ is coming to her, attired in the many-coloured robe of the patriarch Joseph, and waiting to be recognized by her, as he came to Mary of Magdala in the Garden and to the disciples on the Emmaus road on the first Easter Day."

At Jaipur we witnessed Hindus worshiping at sunset in their lovely temple. We were able to release our ingrained fear that somehow we were being unfaithful. When we opened ourselves to experience the adoration and mystery of God with persons whose symbols and rituals were both similar and strange to our own, we were blessed. Here was the offering up of light, the washing with water, the sharing of sacred food, the being marked on the forehead. We embraced the Mystery and gave thanks to God, made known to us in Jesus Christ, both for what is unique and for what connects us with others.

As we walked around the lovely marble temple afterwards, we discovered a four-sided pillar with Jesus Christ, the Madonna and Child, Saint Peter, and Saint Francis of Assissi! On another pillar we found the Buddha. Advaitic Hinduism holds that there is only one Absolute, but there are many windows which help folks experience the Absolute.

In *Pilgrim's Notebook*, David Fleming points out that opening ourselves to signs and symbols of mystery from other cultures and traditions involves letting go of the way we are used to seeing things. This is a call to "enter into a paschal experience not totally unlike that of Jesus who 'emptied himself' in order to assume human experience." Retrieving a term based on the New Testament Greek word for "emptying," David calls this a *kenotic* (self-emptying) spirituality which is incarnational. Incarnational spirituality is embodied in holy particulars from other cultures and traditions as well as from our own. This kenotic and incarnational spirituality embraces Mystery with humility and simplicity. In order to receive the gifts of these stars that fall beyond the limits of our horizons, we have to be willing to color outside the lines!

We drove to San Ildefonso pueblo with Taylor and June McConnell and a group of students on a crisp January evening. We parked outside the village and walked in on the dirt road. In the plaza, piñon and cedar fires had been laid. There were candles in paper bags outlining the roofs of the pueblo houses. The fires were lit and the aroma of the burning wood filled the air with pungent fragrance. The cool breeze of the evening and the presence of the nearby mountains were more than furniture. They became presence for us. Costumed figures emerged from the kivas. The soft sounds of the drum became louder, the dancing began: deer and hunter, bird and bear, pulsing with the presence of the Great Spirit.

It was the eve of the Feast of San Ildefonso. The dancers were blessed in a special service in the Roman Catholic Church. They would spend the night in the hills nearby, and then come down again at dawn to dance at the festival the next day. One of the dancers worked where we were staying. He had given notice months before: "I'm going to dance the festival this year. Preparing for that will be my first priority. I have to prepare my body and my spirit." Although the income from his work was important for his welfare and that of his family, he indicated that he would have to cut back on his hours.

The memory of that night is precious to us. It was clearly holy time in holy space. The connectedness of all things was celebrated. It was not necessary for these people to renounce their Catholic faith in order to celebrate their pueblo spirituality. We were not being unfaithful to Christ to embrace the Mystery with them.

Diana Eck helps us understand that when we are open to the traditions and rituals of persons of different faiths, our own faith is "challenged, changed, and deepened." Acknowledging that we live in a pluralistic world need not lead to relativism. Instead, it calls us to honor diversity and to be clear about our own beliefs and commitments even as we seek to engage in dialogue with those who have different beliefs and practices.

Being open to learn from others, walking with them as we are able with sensitivity and a willingness to learn, and then sharing our journey with them will lead us to a deeper and stronger faith and witness. Once we have "crossed over" into another's world, we will be able to return home—seeing it more clearly than ever before.

So often we are blind to the cultural conditioning supplied by our own perspective. It is as though the form of Christian religion we have received is neutral while the perspectives that come from other cultures pollute or contaminate the purity of our own practices. Embracing Mystery involves renouncing the arrogance that our piece of the sand dollar is the whole thing, that we can color only within the lines given us by our own background and tradition, that stars fall only within the boundaries of our horizon.

Mystery often breaks in upon us by offering us glimpses of God's reign and realm—God's kin-dom. Sometimes these experiences demonstrate the *real presence* of Christ causing that future to break in upon us here and now, weaving the fabric in unforgettable ways. We read in the *New York Times* about weekly protests in Ballymena, a village we had visited in Northern Ireland. Protestant extremists gathered outside the Roman Catholic Church when mass was being celebrated each Saturday evening. They registered an anger and outrage nursed by centuries of misunderstanding and prejudice on both sides. This protest was just one more manifestation of the on-going disputation there. We were disturbed because we had been there, knew that many are suffering, and that some of our closest friends are working hard to establish a just and lasting peace.

When we received an e-mail message several weeks later from our friends, Houston and Roberta McKelvey, we were deeply moved. He wrote about the death and funeral of Roberta's mother, Kathleen. Against the background of the weekly protests, he delighted to note that one-quarter to one-third of the congregation gathered in the Presbyterian church at Ballymena were Roman Catholic. Indeed, Kathleen had her independence in later years only because of the care and support of a Roman Catholic family who lived next door to her. Houston wrote:

> The 33 year-old son of this Roman Catholic family is a man with Down's syndrome, called Damian. He was at the church—big hugs all round. His house and Kathleen's are near the cemetery. As I walked with our son and nephews to the grave, I spotted Damian coming across through the headstones. He broke through the crowd and worked his way in between me and my nephews at the grave side. He was carrying a rose and it was going up and down with a rhythmic action like a baton. To save the young Presbyterian

minister's nerves, I said, "Damian, if that's for Kathleen, you could give it to her now." "There you are, Kathleen," he said, and tossed it into the grave.

I stood with one arm around him and the other round Roberta for the short service of commitment. At the end of it, I had just taken two steps forward to thank the minister, when I heard in the clearest and most sincere of voice, "Hail Mary, full of grace, blessed art thou amongst women and blessed is the fruit of thy womb. . . ." And there was Damian standing at the end of the grave, giving Kathleeen the full works of the Hail Mary.

No one moved. Not a word of criticism has been uttered. Kathleen would have been moved by it and her sense of humor greatly tickled by having the Hail Mary said at her Presbyterian funeral service in Ballymena!

In this vignette, we realize that in a kairotic moment— God's time—a man with the mind of a child transcends the centuries of hatred and violence and proclaims a word of hope. Indeed, Damian embodied the eternal truth of God's grace and love in but a moment of chronos. Damian became a sacrament of the presence of Christ. The power of his witness will never be equaled by all the bombs and guns of extremists on both sides of "the troubles."

Embracing Mystery enables sacramental living to take us where we do not expect to go. The agent of Mystery is the Holy Spirit, blowing where it will, weaving a fabric not only of time and eternity, but also of love and justice and righteousness and peace. Through living our baptism, we are claimed by God "as servants of Christ and stewards of God's mysteries" (1 Cor. 4:1).

Sacramental living moves us to live as sacraments of the Real Presence of Christ in our work and in our worship. All our being and our doing is Eucharist, an "offering of praise and thanksgiving." Together with our companions on the way, we sing with our lips and in our lives:

Come down, O Love divine, seek thou this soul of mine,
and visit it with thine own ardor glowing;
O Comforter, draw near, within my heart appear,
and kindle it, thy holy flame bestowing.

And so the yearning strong, with which the soul will long,
shall far outpass the power of human telling;
for none can guess its grace, till Love create a place
wherein the Holy Spirit makes a dwelling.

Notes
1 Bianco of Siena, trans. Richard F. Littledale, "Come Down, O Love Divine," *The United Methodist Hymnal* (Nashville, Tenn: The United Methodist Publishing House, 1989), 475.

A Guide For Further Exploration:

BIBLIOGRAPHIC ESSAY

We love to read. Some of you may resonate as we do with the piece of folk-wisdom that says, "So many books; so little time!" For some people, reading can be a joy in and of itself as writers invite you to share their insights and experiences. For others, reading is a way to find out things you want to know—you read in order to learn. Many of us are part of both these worlds. Rather than write a book with lots of footnotes, we are opting to share with you something about some of the books we've found helpful and illuminating as a guide for your further exploration.

Both of us have dealt with sacramental living in previous books. Linda reflects on what she learned through the way one family and its congregation handled the tragic death of an eighteen-year old in her book *Rituals for Resurrection: Celebrating Life and Death* (Nashville, Tenn.: Upper Room Books, 1996). Dwight asks "what does it mean to live sacramentally?" in his book on liturgical spirituality, *Food for Pilgrims: A Journey with Saint Luke* (Akron, Ohio: Order of Saint Luke Publications, 1996).

We have used the New Revised Standard Version for all biblical quotations, unless otherwise noted. Study notes in *The New Oxford Annotated Bible* (New York: Oxford University Press, 1991) and *The Harper Collins Study Bible* (New York: HarperCollins, 1993) have provided insights into biblical texts.

This bibliographic guide has grown with the writing of each chapter. We have tried to list books the first time we became aware that they were informing us in our writing (though many of these books are "old friends" and they often influence us without our conscious awareness). Although they circle around and influence us in later chapters, we have listed each book only once.

CHAPTER ONE

Leonardo Boff's *Sacraments of Life, Life of the Sacraments* (Washington, D.C.: The Pastoral Press, 1987) opened a door to a new and more pervasive understanding of sacramentality for us. For a survey of recent developments in sacramental theology, we continue to recommend (and, in the case of our students, to require!) Robert L. Browning and Roy A. Reed, *The Sacraments in Religious Education and Liturgy: An Ecumenical Model* (Birmingham, Ala: Religious Education Press, 1985). The first five chapters of their book are especially relevant for what we have written about in this book.

Bernard Cooke's *Sacraments and Sacramentality*, revised edition (Mystic, Conn.: Twenty-Third Publications, 1994) examines the sacramentality of human experience and finds friendship to be a basic sacrament (along with Christ and the church). We have come to treasure his penetrating insights and deep wisdom both in person and through his writings. For an introduction to historical and contemporary developments from a Roman Catholic perspective, we recommend Kenan B. Osborne, *Sacramental Theology: A General Introduction* (New York: Paulist, 1988). John Baggley's and Richard Temple's *Doors of Perception—Icons and Their Spiritual Significance* (Crestwood, N.Y.: St. Vladimir's Seminary Press, 1988) provides a very helpful introduction to ways in which icons can enrich our spiritual journeys.

For our entire teaching career, we have been recommending Paul Tillich's meaty and extremely helpful little book *Dynamics of Faith* (New York: Harper & Bros., 1958). Here we were introduced to the distinction between sign and symbol. Read slowly and carefully, it changed the way we thought about faith—changes that have stood the test of time and experience.

CHAPTER TWO

Three books that have sensitized us to the centrality of *place* in our spiritual journey are Terry Tempest Williams, *Refuge: An Unnatural History of Family and Place* (New York: Random House, 1992); Carol Brunner Rutledge, *Dying and Living on the Kansas Prairie: A Diary* (Lawrence, Kans: University Press of Kansas, 1994); and Kathleen Norris, *Dakota: A Spiritual Geography* (New York: Houghton Miffin, 1998).

Williams shares her inseparable love for her mother and the love of home with its birds and wetlands of the Great Salt Lake basin in incredibly moving and insightful ways. Her life journey, her own breast cancer, her mother's dying, and the death and life she finds in the bird sanctuaries connected with the fluctuating levels of the Great Salt Lake are integrally interwoven. From her, we can learn much about how God speaks to us when we are attuned to the world around us. Learning to "be still" and to look and listen for God's presence and care can connect us to place so that we are able to tap into own spiritual geographies.

Carol Rutledge knows as well as we do what it feels like to be planted and raised up on the Kansas prairie. Her diary calls us to be open to God's presence and God's message in the landscapes where we are planted. Life and death are to be shaped and shared in the places where we live and work. As we travel to and through death (our own or that of one we love), *place* can be a vehicle for God's grace.

Rina Swentzell's PBS video, *Colores! An Understated Sacredness* (produced and directed by Michael Kamins for KNME-TV, 1991) is a wonderful resource for those who seek to understand the power of place. Rina is a member of a large family of potters from the Santa Clara pueblo; she is an architect and a cultural anthropologist by training and is a deeply spiritual human being. Her book, *Children of Clay: A Family of Pueblo Potters* (Minneapolis, Minn.: Lerner Publishing Group, 1993), is a beautiful way to help children of all ages understand what it means to live into the future by attending to the present while being deeply rooted in the past. We have deep connections to people and to the earth itself. A book that helps us understand the Anasazi (*ancient ones*) is David E. Stuart's *The Magic of Bandelier* (Santa Fe, NMex.: Ancient City Press, 1989).

There are many books dealing with what it means to connect our daily living with being attuned to the spiritual. Among them are Tilden Edwards' *Living Simply Through the Day: Spiritual Survival in a Complex Age* (New York: Paulist, 1998), *Living in the Presence: Spiritual Exercises to Open Your Life to the Awareness of God* (San Francisco: Harper & Row, 1995) and *Sabbath Time: Understanding and Practice for Contemporary Christians* (Nashville: Tenn.: Upper Room Books, 1992); Richard J. Foster's, *Celebration of Discipline: the Path to Spiritual Growth* (San Francisco: HarperSanFrancisco, 1983); and Sue Bender's, *Plain and Simple: A Woman's Journey to the Amish* (San Francisco: HarperSanFrancisco, 1989) and *Everyday Sacred: A Woman's Journey Home* (San Francisco: HarperSanFrancisco, 1995).

CHAPTER THREE

Story has been a carrier of the tradition of faith communities since the time when the Pentateuch (the first five books of the Hebrew Bible) was put into writing; in fact, it began long before that with the oral tradition being shared as stories around a campfire. Thomas H. Groome in *Christian Religious Education: Sharing Our Story and Vision* (San Francisco: Jossey-Bass, 1999) and *Sharing Faith: A Comprehensive Approach to Religious Education* (San Francisco: HarperSanFrancisco, 1991) suggests that transformative teaching and learning takes place when we put our own *stories* in dialogue with the faith *Story* (the Gospel as it comes to us in scripture and tradition) relating to experiences and issues that affect our living. We believe that this is true. Our own life experiences and the stories that inform our own ways of understanding and meaning-sculpting intersect with the power of the Gospel as we know it through the stories of Jesus' life and teaching. When this happens, our eyes may be opened and we may truly know what we see!

Mary Elizabeth Moore's *Education for Continuity & Change: A New Model for Christian Religious Education* (Nashville, Tenn.: Abingdon, 1983) offers many insights regarding ways the *tradition* which tends to be seen as passive can come alive when understood as a *traditioning model* of teaching and learning about faith.

A number of writers now have claimed the power of story as they engage in theological reflection on the stories of their own experience. Several powerful examples of this include Roberta C. Bondi's, *In Ordinary Time: Healing the Wounds of the Heart* (Nashville, Tenn.: Abingdon, 1996) and *Memories of God: Theological Reflections on a Life,* (Nashville, Tenn.: Abingdon, 1995). An especially moving book that tells one's own story within the context of their family's story in such a way that life experience, identity, and one's spiritual journey are woven together is James McBride's *The Color of Water: A Black Man's Tribute to His White Mother* (New York: Riverhead Books, 1996).

Understanding the ways in which rituals may grow out of our life experiences—our stories—is being made clear in books like Tad W. Guzie's *The Book of Sacramental Basics* (Mahwah, N.J.: Paulist, 1982) and Don E. Saliers' *Worship Come to Its Senses* (Nashville, Tenn.: Abingdon, 1996). Henri J. M. Nouwen's *Can You Drink the Cup?* (Notre Dame, Ind.: Ave Maria, 1996) is both simple and profound.

On a more theoretical level, the chapter on "Ritual and Verbal Image" in *Unsearchable Riches: The Symbolic Nature of Liturgy* by David N. Power (New York: Pueblo Publishing Co., 1984) is a good place to begin. Catherine Bell's *Ritual Theory; Ritual Practice* (New York: Oxford University Press, 1992) provides a more comprehensive analysis for those who wish to dig deeper. Any thoughtful reflection on ritual today must take into account the seminal work of Victor Turner. In *The Forest of Symbols: Aspects of Ndembu Ritual* (Ithaca, N.Y.: Cornell University Press, 1970) he traces the model of ritual in relation to his own research in Africa. One of the best summaries of Turner's approach can be found in *Celebration: Studies in Festival and Ritual,* edited by him (Washington, D.C.: Smithsonian Institution, 1982).

What connecting rituals and life experience may mean for those of us who work with children is addressed by Elizabeth Francis Caldwell in *Come unto Me: Rethinking the Sacraments for Children* (Cleveland, Ohio: Pilgrim, 1996) and by Gretchen Wolff Pritchard in *Offering the Gospel to Children* (Boston, Mass.: Cowley Publications, 1992).

A fine book of resources for creating ritual that speaks to and has healing power for life's journeys is Mari West Zimmerman's *Take and Make Holy* (Chicago: Liturgy Training Publications, 1995).

CHAPTER FOUR

Gunilla Norris' powerful book, *Being Home: A Book of Meditations* (New York: Crown, 1991) helps us see that as we cross thresholds "the entire past" rushes to meet "the endless future." Her use of common, ordinary experiences as metaphors are recast in poetic form in ways that connect everyday objects and routines with the ways we sculpt meaning and faith across time and space.

Two very different but excellent books which focus on weaving time and space into our everyday journeys in faith are Frederic and Mary Ann Brussat's *Spiritual Literacy: Reading the Sacred in Everyday Life* (New York: Simon and Schuster, 1998) and a book edited by Dorothy C. Bass, *Practicing Our Faith: A Way of Life for a Searching People* (San Francisco: Jossey-Bass, 1998).

The Brussats include quotations from an amazing range of printed resources—from Maya Angelou to Thich Nhat Hanh and from Jane Smiley to Howard Thurman. They organize the book around their own "alphabet of spiritual literacy" (from *a=attention* to *z=zeal*) and around topics including things, places, nature, animals, leisure, creativity, service, body, relationships, and community.

Dorothy Bass' book invites readers to focus on twelve "central Christian practices"—honoring the body, hospitality, household economics, saying yes and saying no, keeping sabbath, testimony, discernment, shaping communities, forgiveness, healing, dying well and singing our lives. Growing out of the belief that people at the dawn of the twenty-first century are yearning for "deeper understanding of and involvement in the redemptive practice of God in the world," this book blends personal life experiences with insights from those disciplines of study that help us understand our lives—especially philosophy, history, sociology, and theology.

Both of these books are well worth the investment of time and money. In them, readers will be invited to reflect on their own journeys as they engage the myriad of ideas and journeys that are found painted on the pages of these books.

Nourishing the Soul: Discovering the Sacred in Everyday Life (San Francisco: HarperSanFrancisco, 1995) edited by Anne Simpkinson, Charles Simpkinson, and Rose Solari is a provacative book of essays reflecting on how a culture which appears to have "lost its soul" while giving most attention to "the pursuit of the outer life, . . . money, convenience, and the illusion of immortality" might refocus on the inner life and nourish its soul. Contributors range from Thomas Moore to Jim Wallis and Rosemary Radford Ruether.

155

Henri J. M. Nouwen's *Here and Now: Living in the Spirit* (New York: Crossroad, 1994) is a deceptively simple book that has the ability to go to the heart. His earlier book, *Reaching Out: The Three Movements of the Spiritual Life* (Garden City, N.Y.: Doubleday, 1986) continues to be helpful. For those who find Father Nouwen's work nourishing, the earlier spiritual journals will be of great interest: *The Genesee Diary: Report from a Trappist Monastary* (Garden City, N.Y.: Image, 1981; *¡Gracias!, A Latin American Journal* (San Francisco: Harper & Row, 1983); *The Road to Daybreak: A Spiritual Journey* (New York: Doubleday, 1990); and the posthumously published *Sabbatical Journey: The Diary of His Final Year* (New York: Crossroad, 1998).

Anne Morrow Lindbergh's classic, *Gift from the Sea* (New York: Pantheon Books, 1955, 1997 ed.), shares her ways of weaving the timelessness of the messages conveyed to those who walk the beach and *listen* to the shells with which it gifts us.

CHAPTER FIVE

Gunilla Norris's *Becoming Bread: Meditations on Loving and Transformation* (New York: Crown, 1993) is both simple and profound as her poetry explores all that is involved in making (and becoming) bread. It bears reading, rereading, and would be useful for small groups to use to engage in prayerful reflection together, as well as for individual devotional reading. *Mother Teresa: A Simple Path* compiled by Lucinda Vardey (New York: Ballantine Books, 1995) is a wonderfully touching reflection on lives lived with the belief that "every act of love is a prayer." Maria Harris's *Proclaim Jubilee! A Spirituality for the Twenty-First Century* (Louisville, Ky.: Westminster John Knox, 1996) offers readers a way to immerse themselves in God's living Word as they move into the twenty-first century—giving and receiving forgiveness and embracing a spirituality that is embodied in all of our relationships as we seek "jubilee justice" for the whole world.

CHAPTER SIX

Another video in the Colores series is *Michael Naranjo* (Derry, N.H.: Chip Taylor Communications, 1994). It is a powerful presentation of Naranjo's life and work as a sculptor. His insight far exceeds that of many sighted persons. It is an excellent resource for those who want to reflect on the deeper meanings of darkness and light, and of what it means to truly see.

Richard Bresnahan introduced us to *Another Turn of the Crank* by Wendell Berry (Washington, D.C.: Counterpoint, 1996). Berry's concern with the use of sustainable and renewable resources is akin to Richard's own perspective.

Developing Nathan Mitchell's basic insights, Robert Brooks uses striking images and perceptive commentary to reflect on the meaning of the Easter Vigil in his chapter on "Post-Baptismal Catechesis" in *The Baptismal Mystery and the Catechumenate*, edited by Michael W. Merriman (New York: Church Publishing, 1990). David Regan opens up for us the possibilities for helping Christians reflect on their experiences of Word and Sacrament in *Experience the Mystery: Pastoral Possibilities for Christian Mystagogy* (Collegeville, Minn: The Liturgical Press, 1994). He uses an ancient word to refer to an approach which we have taken in writing much of this book: *mystagogy*. It is a concept that is being reclaimed in the approach to adult baptism described in *Come to the Waters* by Daniel T. Benedict (Nashville, Tenn.: Discipleship Resources, 1997). For us, mystagogy is the process of drawing out the deep, rich, and inexhaustible meaning in the worship of the church—particularly in the sacraments. For mystagogy the goal is to love as well as understand the sacraments and God's Word in Christ which they celebrate.

One approach to the Easter Vigil can be found under sections 368 to 376 of *The United Methodist Book of Worship* (Nashville, Tenn: The United Methodist Publishing House, 1992). Other services for the Easter Vigil (The Great Vigil) are available in the worship resources of many denominations, including *The Book of Common Prayer* (New York: The Church Hymnal Corporation, 1979), 285–295.

CHAPTER SEVEN

The pioneering work of Odo Casel can be found in *The Mystery of Christian Worship and Other Writings*, first published in 1932. An English translation was published in 1962 (Westminster, Md.: Newman). Casel's work is summarized and developed in the chapter on "The Liturgy: Mystery of Worship" in I. H. Dalmais, *Introduction to the Liturgy* (Baltimore, Md.: Helicon Press, 1961). The distinction between problem and mystery can be found in Gabriel Marcel, *The Mystery of Being* (London: Harvill Press, 1950). Chapter 10 is especially helpful. For a commentary on Marcel, Dwight returned to a book he used years ago in teaching philosophy: Francis J. Lescoe's *Existentialism With or Without God*, new edition (New York: Alba House, 1974). He continues to find it a helpful introduction to existentialist thinkers.

Any discussion of our experience of the sacred today is influenced by Rudolf Otto's classic work, first published in 1917, *The Idea of the Holy* (New York: Oxford University Press, 1958). A delightful and profound introduction by way of fiction is the chapter "The Piper at the Gates of Dawn" in Kenneth Grahame's *The Wind in the Willows* (Our favorite illustrated version is published in New York by Holt, Rinerhart and Winston, 1980).

Our horizons have been broadened and our spirituality deepened by the work of two very different persons: Henri le Saux, the Belgium Benedictine better known by his Indian name—Abhishiktānanda, and Diana L. Eck, a United Methodist from Montana who has been able to introduce many to the religions of India. The quotations of Abhishiktānanda Fr. Henrile Saux found in chapter seven come from his *Guru and Disciple* (London: SPCK, 1974), which provides a fascinating introduction to his thinking in narrative form. His *Hindu-Christian Meeting Point* (Delhi, India: ISPCK, 1976; rev. ed.) presents his theological perspective, and *Saccidananda* (Delhi, India: ISPCK, 1984; revised ed.) provides a depth dialogue between Christianity and Hinduism in terms of "spirituality." His best known book is *Prayer* (London: SPCK, 1972; revised ed; also published by Westminster, 1973) that continues to be a classic of contemporary Christian devotion.

Diana L. Eck's *Encountering God: A Spiritual Journey from Bozeman to Banaras* (Boston, Mass.: Beacon, 1994) is an amazing book, opening new vistas of understanding for us and for our students. Perhaps it is because she shares our denominational background (though those from other backgrounds have found it helpful too), but this is on our you-really-must-read-this list. If you want to get beneath the surface tourists see and get some feeling of the depth behind an ancient holy city of India, read Diana L. Eck's *Banaras: City of Light* (New York: Columbia University Press, 1982).

Father David A. Fleming uses his experiences in India to reflect on incarnation and inculturation in his chapter "In the Heart of the World" in *Pilgrim's Notebook: An Experience of Religious Life* (Maryknoll, N.Y.: Orbis, 1992). It is also a good introduction to the nature of life in a religious order.

Ongoing nourishment for our spiritual pilgrimage has been provided by four periodicals: *Sacramental Life, Weavings, Alive Now,* and *Sojourners.* Each provides a particular perspective and has its unique flavor.

These resources provide insight and direction. We hope our writing has encouraged you to "mine your own experiences," tell your own stories, and make your own connections with sacramental living. You are a crucial resource who must not be overlooked. May the amazing grace of our Lord Jesus Christ, the abounding love of God, and the sustaining presence of the Holy Spirit be with you on your journey. May God be with us and with all peoples as we seek to heal the earth and to work and pray: "Your kin-dom come."

ABOUT THE AUTHORS

Dwight W. Vogel

Dwight W. Vogel is Professor of Theology and Ministry and Director of the Nellie B. Ebersole Program in Sacred Music at Garrett-Evangelical Theological Seminary, Evanston, Illinois. Prior to that he was the pastor of St. Luke's United Methodist Church in Dubuque, Iowa. He is an elder in the Iowa Annual Conference.

Having grown up in Kansas, Dr. Vogel taught for twenty years at Westmar College. He is the Abbot of the Order of St. Luke—a religious order in the United Methodist Church dedicated to sacramental and liturgical scholarship, education, and practice. He writes extensively on the spiritual life including books, articles, and curriculum resources. His books include *Food for Pilgrims, The Daily Office,* and *By Water and the Spirit.*

He holds degrees from Westmar College (B.A.), Boston University (A.M.), Andover Newton Theological School (B.D.), and Northwestern University (Ph.D.).

Linda J. Vogel

Linda J Vogel is Professor of Christian Education at Garrett-Evangelical Theological Seminary. Prior to that she was minister of education at St. Luke's United Methodist Church in Dubuque, Iowa. She is a deacon in full connection in the Iowa annual conference.

With Dwight, she taught at Westmar College for twenty years and was Director of Continuing Education. Dr. Vogel is the author of numerous articles and curriculum resources. Her books include *Helping a Child Understand Death, Religious Education of Older Adults, Teaching and Learning in Communities of Faith: Empowering Adults through Religious*

159

Education, and *Rituals for Resurrection* published by Upper Room Books.

She holds degrees from Boston University (B.S.), Andover-Newton Theological School (M.R.E.), and the University of Iowa (Ph.D.).

Dwight and Linda have been married for forty years and are the parents of three adult children. They have three grand-children and three great-grandchildren. They feel equally at home in the beautiful Black Hills of South Dakota and in the city of Chicago. Dwight and Linda invite all who journey toward sacramental living with them to join in caring for the earth and in working for justice-love so that all children are safe and well-fed. Let us create a church where all God's children are invited to the welcome-Table. Together let us invite everyone to join in working to bring God's kin-dom on earth.